VICTORIOUS

Living a life of complete freedom and victory in Christ

---

by
Barry Tallis

VICTORIOUS: Living a life of complete freedom and victory in Christ.

Copyright © 2016 Nourish Ministries, LLC.

PUBLISHED BY: NOURISH MINISTRIES
www.nourishministries.com

All rights reserved. No part of this book may be reproduced or transmitted in any form or by any means without written permission from the author. The use of short quotations or occasional page copying for personal or group study is permitted and encouraged. Permission will be granted upon request. Unless otherwise identified, Scripture quotations are from The Holy Bible: English Standard Version. (2001). Wheaton: Standard Bible Society. Used by permission.

Scripture quotations marked KJV are from the King James Version of the Bible.

Scripture quotations marked NAS are from the New American Standard Bible, copyright © 1960, 1962, 1963, 1968, 1971, 1972, 1973, 1975, 1977, 1995 by The Lockman Foundation. Used by permission. (www.Lockman.org)

Scripture quotations marked NIV are taken from the Holy Bible, New International Version®, NIV®. Copyright © 1973, 1978, 1984, 2011 by Biblica, Inc.™ Used by permission of Zondervan. All rights reserved worldwide. www.zondervan.com The "NIV" and "New International Version" are trademarks registered in the United States Patent and Trademark Office by Biblica, Inc.™

ISBN: 978-0692738245

SPECIAL SALES:
Pastors, churches, and ministry leaders can receive special discounts when purchasing VICTORIOUS resources. For more info, please email info@nourishministries.com

ACKNOWLEDGEMENTS

To my loving family. May this book be a testimony to the power and authority we have in Jesus Christ, His transforming power to take a man like me and raise him up victoriously. May this book arm you with the wisdom and knowledge to be strong soldiers for His kingdom.

To Brian and Robbi, J.D. and Shawna, Cody, and Pastor Clyde for your ministry and instruction in spiritual warfare.

To Pastor Keith for mentoring me and encouraging me in pursuing all He has for us in the Kingdom.

TABLE OF CONTENTS

Chapter One - Introduction 7

PART ONE: WARFARE

Chapter Two - The Enemy 14
Chapter Three - Battlefield 36
Chapter Four - Enemy Tactics 46
Chapter Five - Strongholds 56
Chapter Six - Restoring the Foundation 69

PART TWO: THE BATTLES

Chapter Seven - Learning from the Past 80
Chapter Eight - Gideon 88
Chapter Nine - Ahaz & Hezekiah 101
Chapter Ten - Jericho 119
Chapter Eleven - Amalek 130

PART THREE: THE KINGS

Chapter Twelve - Kings 142
Chapter Thirteen - Kings & Priests 147
Chapter Fourteen - Fallen Kings 157
Chapter Fifteen - Stronger 170
Chapter Sixteen - Prayer 178

PART FOUR: VICTORY

Chapter Seventeen - Victory 188
Chapter Eighteen - Arise 198
Chapter Nineteen - Authority 215
Chapter Twenty - Battle Plan 244
References 255

CHAPTER ONE - INTRODUCTION

"Now these things happened to them as an example, but they were written down for our instruction, on whom the end of the ages has come."
1 Corinthians 10:11

God wants us to live victorious lives. But many of us are unaware we are in a battle or how to fight from a position of victory. Have you ever thought about what it takes to have a joyous, successful, fulfilled life?

God desires for us to live a life full of victory. He doesn't want us to just "wade through life" until we go to heaven. He has given us His divine nature to move from a position of defeat to a position of victory. VICTORIOUS is designed to give you insight and direction on how to live this life. This book is for people who are tired of letting the enemy of this world triumph in their life, causing them to be disconnected and separated from God, even while sitting in the seats at church.

In my life, I have experienced the difference between living a victorious life in Christ and living a life where I struggled daily with the enemy's lies about me. I have broken free of the enemy's grasp on me, and I have had the privilege to guide others through this process.

Jesus said that He came that we may have life, and have it more abundantly (John 10:10). Have you received that promise? People I have guided who struggled to feel accepted, felt defeated daily by sin, or struggled with doubt, fears, and anger, found true freedom in Christ through the principles outlined in this book.

Living a victorious life involves knowing who our enemy is, understanding his tactics, learning from the past to gain the upper hand, rising up in our authority in Jesus Christ, and walking out our victory with practical biblical steps.

By implementing the principles and truths detailed in this book, many people have come to realize the truth that the battle is already won and have started living in the victory out on a daily basis.

Overview of the Battle

One thing I want you to remember is that the battle has already been won. We just need to start living it out on a daily basis. But we need to know what led up to this victory and why we, nevertheless, need to be prepared for battle.

It all began when God created the angels. Lucifer, the anointed angel, rebelled against God and was cast out of heaven along with one-third of the angels. (Revelation 12:9)

God then created man, in His image, a little lower than the angels. (Genesis 1:26-27 and Hebrews 2:7)

Satan started fighting back against God's divine plan by deceiving Adam and Eve, which led to the first to sin. (Genesis 3:1-8)

God is always bringing His creation back to Him. God countered Satan's move by providing a redemptive covering for Adam and Eve so they could return back to fellowship with Him. (Genesis 3:21)

Satan made his next move by encouraging Cain to kill Abel to sever the godly line. But God responded to Satan through Seth's birth, making a way for humanity to call once again upon the name of the Lord. (Genesis 4:1-8, 25-26)

Satan countered that move by luring Nimrod and his kingdom to build a tower thinking they could make themselves as high as the heavens. (Genesis 11:1-4)

God turned His gaze onto a man named Abraham and called out a nation through him to be set apart and made holy. Satan, however, countered that plan by trapping this nation in Egypt under Pharaoh's rule. (Genesis 12:1-6)

But then God protected and rose up Moses in the midst of Pharaoh's rule, putting him in high standing in Egypt. Satan allowed anger to overtake Moses, and he murdered an Egyptian. In exile in Midian, God called Moses to deliver the nation of Israel from the bondage of slavery. Through signs and wonders, God used Moses to deliver His chosen nation.

Throughout the rest of the Old Testament, we see a nation being reconciled by God and pulled away by Satan's tactics. By the end of the Old Testament, there was a period of over 400 years where we have no biblically recorded move by either side.

When the New Testament begins, we see God place His own Son, Jesus Christ, on the battlefield. (Matthew 1-3)

Satan strived to tempt Jesus in the wilderness, just as he had tempted Adam in the garden. Jesus, however, overcame Satan's deceptions and lies through the Word of God. (Matthew 4:1-17)

Satan used the legalistic religious people of that day to arrange the crucifixion of Jesus Christ. But Satan miscalculated. He didn't realize that death on the cross was not the end. It was, in fact, simply a setup for the final move that God would make by raising Jesus from the dead. (Matthew 26-28)

The accomplishment of the cross and the resurrection of Christ was God's final move in a battle of the ages and offered each one of us victory over an enemy who is seeking to intimidate, deceive, and destroy us. The ultimate winner of this battle has been decided.

LIVE THE VICTORIOUS LIFE

You can live a life free from the enemy, from the constant attacks on your mind, body, and soul. You do not need to struggle another day with habitual sin. You can be free from it and the shame, guilt, and self-condemnation. As you read VICTORIOUS, you will experience a deeper connection to God, Jesus, and the Holy Spirit.

Do not continue living another day in defeat. Be the person God called you to be and step into the battle armed with the knowledge and wisdom to defeat your enemy. Why struggle another day not being effective in His kingdom. Rise up and take your rightful place as sons of God.

Victory has been secured. While you and I are on earth and still battling, Satan, a defeated enemy, still has not accepted the terms of surrender and continues to use his tactics to make us believe we are defeated. We need to live in light of the truth of the victory gained through the resurrection of Jesus Christ. Because of His death & resurrection, Satan no longer has authority over you to defeat you. His only means to overcome you is to deceive you—to make you believe that the winner of the battle is yet undecided. This battle is called spiritual warfare.

One of the tactics that Satan uses is called strongholds. Strongholds are thoughts and beliefs built upon lies that Satan has fed us. The way to tear down strongholds is with focusing on and learning the truth found in God's Word, and not on the lies enemy has been trying to get us to believe. If the enemy has been feeding us a lie, we need to stop believing the lie and counter the lie with God's truth, found in His word. In Ephesians 6:17 (ESV) "...*the sword of the Spirit, which is the word of God.*" is the weapon we use to tear down these strongholds. Strongholds are the enemy's favorite tactic in the war against our soul.

There were many battles that God's people fought that did not end in victory. Only when the nation of Israel trusted obeyed God did they emerge victorious. The same is true in our lives today. We face battles, not with swords and spears, but in our mind, will, and emotions.

We will be victorious when we are obedient to what God's truth reveals to us. Many times people complain they do not see victories in their lives. However, they are also ignoring the fact that they are not obedient to God's word. They also could be suffering the consequences of past disobedience, even though they fully trust in the Lord. While we have forgiveness of sins, many of us are still living with the consequences of the sin.

Just as a soldier in the natural world improves his skills by studying the historical, geographical, and cultural record of previous battles, we can develop our spiritual warfare abilities by studying decisive battles of the Bible and live a victorious life.

Let's examine Satan's tactics so we can defend against them, learn from the battles past, and more importantly, raise up champions who will not walk around defeated.

It is time to be VICTORIOUS!

PART ONE
WARFARE

CHAPTER TWO - THE ENEMY

I believed a lie. I was told I wasn't good enough, that I wasn't talented and that I will not amount to so much in life. Believe me, all those lies are a reminder that there is a very real enemy—the devil. He is the enemy of your soul. His intention is to cripple you with lies he plants in your heart before you know the difference between right and wrong, or good and bad, and before you learn to take responsibility your life, by choosing to either believe his lies or believing God's truth.

God who is all-wise pre-empted Satan's activities by giving us His word contained in the book called the Bible. In the Bible, God tells us to be aware of Satan's possible attack at any moment. In one statement contained in about two verses in the Bible, God told us to: *"Be self controlled and alert. Your enemy the devil prowls around like a roaring lion looking for someone to devour. Resist him, firm in your faith, knowing that the same kinds of suffering are being experienced by your brotherhood throughout the world."* 1 Peter 5:8–9 (ESV).

Now, I need you to know that the devil, your enemy, does actually exist. By that, I mean you have an enemy who is against you and will come against you with all the weapons in his armory. I want to state here that there are two opposite extremes regarding attention given to the devil, and he is happy with either. Again, this is one of his strategies of getting people in a corner where he can always pray on their ignorance.

At one extreme are people who are a bit too preoccupied with Satan, constantly worrying about him, and looking behind every corner for him to see whether he is hanging around. The end of such people is usually an interest in the occult. There is a danger in being interested in the things pertaining to the occult. These people can be overly focused on the enemy and end up trying to diagnose every illness or mental disorder as a case of demon possession.

The second extreme are those who forget about Satan completely, or worse, deny his existence. He *"has blinded the minds of the unbelievers, to keep them from seeing the light of the gospel"* 2 Corinthians 4:4 (ESV). They dismiss every efforts of attacking him, even to the point of neglecting what the Bible says about him.

There is an intelligent being that stands behind all the evils of the world, and his name is Satan, the devil. His chief aim and design in this world are to defeat Christ's purposes, or at least to oppose, hinder or delay God's purposes for you and me. He started out on this course right from the creation and went after it more aggressively with the advent of the birth of Christ. Satan is not a novice. He knew that Jesus was God's Son (Matthew 4:3) and that Jesus was the Holy One of God (Mark 1:23-24). Therefore, he went after Jesus to kill Him even before He fulfilled the purpose for which He was born (Matthew 2:16-18, 4:6) and eventually did so through Judas Iscariot (John 13:2)

Now it will be well for us to look at what God's Word says about Satan - who he is, how he came to be, and most importantly how to be on guard against him.

Satan

Satan is known by many names throughout the works of history. These names are diverse, and the meaning of each one points to his character, purpose, and desire. We MUST keep this in mind. It is a pity that so often we overlook and push aside the name Satan, which is chief among the many of his names. That ought not to be so. We need to understand that he's not a little red caricature with a pitchfork and a pointy tail., We must realize that he is so much more than a caricature He operates much more covertly in our day-to-day lives.

From what we read in Scripture, we come to understand that Satan was originally one of the mightiest princes of the angelic world. He was a leader in the heavenly realm, and as such remained that leader of those who revolted with him and fell away from God (See Revelation 12:7-12). In revolting against God, one of the names associated with Satan is "the Adversary." And he is not just the adversary of man, but also an adversary of God, first and foremost.

Satan challenged God in heaven and continues to do so here on earth. He started out by challenging God's handiwork in attacking Adam and causing the first sin to enter into the world, which was perfect, without sin, before that time. Thus, his destructive work earned him the name "the Destroyer" or Apollyon. After the entrance of sin into the world, he became "the Accuser", or in Greek, Diabolos, accusing God's people continually as stated in Revelation 12:10: *"For the accuser of our brothers and sisters, who accuses them before our God day and night."*

To this day, he remains the leader of the angelic hosts, which were cast down with him in his fall, and he continues to employ them in their resistance to Christ and His Kingdom. Jesus often referred to Satan as the *"Prince of this world"* (John 12:31, 14:30, and 16:11) and even the *"god of this world"* 2 Corinthians 4:4. Notice the use of the word "of THIS world" and not "of THE world." The means that he is not in control of the world, for God is in control, and God has given all authority to Christ. But it does convey that Satan is in control of the evil world, in so far as it is ethically separated from God.

In Ephesians 2:2 (NKJV), Satan is called *"the prince of the power of the air, the spirit that is now at work in the sons of disobedience."*

Now, it is important that we know that although Satan is supernatural, he is not divine. He has a lot of power and influence, but is not omnipotent and such operates on a restricted scale. In summary, Satan is a "spiritual, supernatural being who opposed God and continues to oppose Him and seeks to disrupt the plans and purposes of God's people and lead them astray and into rebellion against God."

THE ACCUSER

The actual name "Satan" appears clearly in a couple of passages in the Old Testament, the majority written in the Hebrew language. The Hebrew word "Satan" is translated as "the accuser". Thus, Satan is described as an "angel" who acts as the accuser or adversary.

In Zechariah 3:1–2, Satan appears in the heavenly court, standing at the right side of Joshua, the high priest, to accuse him.

Again in the first two chapters of Job, Satan appears among *"the sons of God"* to accuse Job and then to afflict Job, but within limits imposed by God (Job 1:12; 2:6).

Again, in 1 Chronicles 21:1 he appears and encourages David to go against God's will. In this case, we see the enemy not standing and accusing God's people, but tempting them to go against God's plan. This was the tactic he first used at the beginning of human history with Adam and Eve, which eventually their fall and to Adam's accusation of Eve before God.

THE SERPENT

In Genesis 3:1, we learn of the "serpent" that tempted Eve in the Garden of Eden. Have you ever wondered why, of all the animals that could have been used by Satan to inhabit, he choose the serpent?

"Serpent" is the general term for "snake." In many non-biblical ancient myths, texts, and relics, the serpent is represented as an object of both reverence and of disdain. The serpent conveyed ambivalent meanings of life, death, chaos, and wisdom. In ancient Near Eastern imagery, the serpent is depicted as the one directly opposed to creation, representing a powerful force that opposes the creator-god.

These same meanings associated with the serpent are seen as well in biblical texts. The rejuvenating effects of Moses' bronze serpent (Numbers 21:8; cf. 2 Kings 18:4) and its respected shrewdness (Matthew 10:16). The serpent's venomous death (e.g., Psalm 58:4), the divine opponent (Isaiah 27:1), and its hostile opposition to the woman and her seed (Genesis 3:15).

Though the snake is never identified as Satan in Genesis, the characteristics of the snake as an adversary of God, and his plan of deceiving Adam and Eve, and of destroying the pristine and perfect world that God created points clearly to the nature of Satan!

ANCIENT RELIGIOUS TEXTS

While we fully believe that the Bible is the true source of knowledge and wisdom, it is worth evaluating the religious writings of the Jewish culture that are not included in the canonized scriptures, but are considered known and trusted sources within the Jewish faith

The Jews developed the idea of Satan during the intertestamental period, also calling him Belial, Mastema, and Samuel. The intertestamental period is the gap of time between the period covered by the Hebrew Bible and the period covered by the Christian New Testament. It is commonly believed to cover over roughly four hundred years, spanning the ministry of Malachi (c. 420 BC) to the appearance of John the Baptist in the early 1st century AD[1].

In the Jewish texts of Jubilees and 1 Enoch, Satan appears in the roles of tempting people, of accusing them in heaven before God, and of hindering God's saving plan. Within the Dead Sea Scrolls, Satan (Belial) is identified as the leader of the evil forces and attacker of the righteous. In some of these Jewish, non-canonized texts, Satan is often identified with stories from the biblical Old Testament in which his name was formerly absent. In the Book of Wisdom, he is designated as the one who caused the fall. In Jubilees, he is recognized as the one who controls the angels who fell and are referenced in Genesis 6:1-4. In 2 Enoch, Satan is identified as a fallen angel himself.

Again, we are not suggesting that any form of doctrine should be created from these references, but it does serve to illustrate the reality and characteristics of our enemy. From the Old Testament, we see a scattering of ideas and themes that reference Satan, but no formal doctrine is created.

New Testament

However, the New Testament does develop a doctrine, a codification of beliefs or taught principles, of Satan. There are many names and translations of Satan (Hebrew for "accuser"), the devil (the Greek translation of Satan), Beliar, Beelzebul, the Adversary, the Dragon, the Enemy, the Serpent, the Tester, and the Wicked One.

The doctrine of Satan is based primarily on the words of Jesus and those of his apostles/disciples.

Satan depicted as the ruler of a host of angels. Jesus describes the reality of those who make Jesus their Lord and Savior and those who follow Satan in Matthew 25:41 (NKJV): *"Depart from me, you cursed, into the eternal fire prepared for the devil and his angels."*

In Luke 4, we see Jesus on the eve of the launch of his ministry tempted in the desert by the devil. Satan states that he would give Jesus *"all their authority and splendor; it has been given to me"* Luke 4:6 (NIV). Jesus doesn't correct this statement and authority by Satan, but rebukes him and states that His true purpose and that of man is to *"Worship God and serve him only"* Luke 4:8 (NIV).

In Acts 26:18, Apostle Paul pleads his commissioning mandate from Jesus to those listening to him that God's purpose through him is to *"open their eyes, so that they may turn from darkness to light and from the power of Satan to God, that they may receive forgiveness of sins and a place among those who are sanctified by faith".* Paul, a devoted student of Jesus Christ, knew and experienced firsthand the teachings of Jesus about the devil.

To the Corinthian church, the Apostle Paul describes those who are not receptive to the gospel and are perishing thus: *"In their case the god of this world has blinded the minds of the unbelievers, to keep them from seeing the light of the gospel of the glory of Christ, who is the image of God"* 2 Corinthians. 4:4 (NIV). He stated that our enemy has blinded those who do not know the Lord and seeks to keep them from knowing and understanding the freedom that is in Jesus Christ.

The reality of our adversary is evident throughout Scripture. We must strive to understand the complete picture of our enemy if we are to remain vigilant to his attacks to keep us from fully experiencing and operating in God's love, power, and authority.

LEADER OF FALLEN ANGELS

Satan is identified on numerous occasions in the Scriptures as the leader of a fallen group of angels from the heavenly realm.

The demons that are mentioned in the Bible are the angels who rebelled with Satan. In Matthew 12:24, Satan is designated the prince of the demons indicating that since their leader, Satan, is an angel, the demons must also be angels, yet fallen and against God.

Satan has well-organized ranks of angels who assist him in his plan and purposes of deceiving the nations. Two of these positions are "rulers and authorities", which are the same name used for two of the classes of good angels referenced in Ephesians 3:10 and Ephesians 6:12. This may indicate that the same kinds of beings make up the personnel of angels, and therefore that these evil beings are fallen angels. Ephesians 6:12 (ESV) states: *"For we do not wrestle against flesh and blood, but against the rulers, against the authorities, against the cosmic powers over this present darkness, against the spiritual forces of evil in the heavenly places."*

Demons were the reality behind ancient gods of the people as seen in Deuteronomy 32:17; Psalm 106:37; 1 Corinthians 10:20). Similarly, they are also propagators of false doctrine: *"In later times some will abandon the faith and follow deceiving spirits and things taught by demons"* 1 Timothy 4:1 (NIV).

In several places in the New Testament, demons are called spirits, or unclean spirits, which connects them with the spirit world of angels, not humans. The demon referred to in Matthew 17:1, for example, is called an unclean spirit in the parallel account in Mark 9:25. The corresponding mention of demons and spirits is found in Luke 10:17–20. In Matthew 8:16, Jesus healed many demon-possessed people by casting out the unclean spirits from them.

Demons are fallen angels, immortal creatures serving Satan. Having joined Satan's rebellion, they were cast out of heaven to await final judgment. Their minds are permanently set to oppose God, His goodness, truth, the kingdom of Christ, and the welfare of human beings. They have real but limited power and freedom of movement. They are not omniscient, omnipresent, or omnipotent, nor are they biblically portrayed as being able to read our thoughts. We also can say that some illnesses and afflictions are from demons, but not all. This is because Jesus did not rebuke demons every time he healed a person.

Most importantly, however, is that the New Testament teaches us that Satan has been evil from the beginning. *"The one who does what is sinful is of the devil, because the devil has been sinning from the beginning. The reason the Son of God appeared was to destroy the devil's work"* 1 John 3:8 (NIV).

The fallen angels, including Satan, will ultimately be fully disarmed by Jesus Christ. He has delivered us from them and transferred us to His kingdom (Col 1:13 and 2:15). We see the culmination of this full disarmament in Revelation 12:7-9:

> *"Now war arose in heaven, Michael and his angels fighting against the dragon. And the dragon and his angels fought back, but he was defeated, and there was no longer any place for them in heaven. And the great dragon was thrown down, that ancient serpent, who is called the devil and Satan, the deceiver of the whole world—he was thrown down to the earth, and his angels were thrown down with him."*

Desire of Satan

Satan and his army are clearly against all that is created by God. But the question is what caused this enmity in Satan, a once highly esteemed angel of God? We get a glimpse of what caused his fall in a Hebrew prophetic speech that the prophet Isaiah spoke over a king of Babylon. It was not too uncommon to use a description of a human event to parallel a description of a heavenly event, in a limited way.

How you have fallen from heaven, morning star, son of the dawn!
You have been cast down to the earth, you who once laid low the nations!
You said in your heart,
"I will ascend to the heavens;
I will raise my throne above the stars of God;
I will sit enthroned on the mount of assembly, on the utmost heights of Mount Zaphon.
I will ascend above the tops of the clouds;
I will make myself like the Most High."
Isaiah 14:12-14 (NIV)

The term "morning star" is translated in Latin as Lucifer, which became a common name for Satan used by the early church. It also gives us a clue into some of his tactics and insight into his plot against God. In Revelation 22:16, the same title "morning star" is given to Jesus Christ. Since the same title is being referred to both Satan and Jesus, we can see that one of Satan's tactics is to counterfeit the plan of God as a pseudo-Christ. We will look more into this in the following chapters.

We see five "I will" statements in Isaiah 14 that describes the desire of Satan that led to his rebellion against God.

1. I will ascend to heaven.
2. I will raise my throne above the stars of God.
3. I will sit on the mount of assembly in the recesses of the north.
4. I will ascend above the heights of the clouds.
5. I will make myself like the Most High.

As an angel, Satan had access to all of heaven and had great power and responsibility there. As if that was not enough, he started nurturing a desire to have equality with God in heaven and to rule over the angels. He wanted the glory that belonged to God and wanted all of heaven to worship him. He coveted the position of God. He wanted the authority and control that rightfully belongs to God. His sin and ultimate downfall were due to his direct challenge to the power and authority of God.

BIBLICAL REALITY

Our enemy is real. As we look to our Lord and Savior to grow in righteousness and sanctification, we can look to Him to understand the reality He faced when dealing with Satan and his army of fallen angels.

I have heard countless stories of great spiritual leaders of our time running into opposition, roadblocks, illness, etc. just as they were about to accomplish great things for the Kingdom. Many were ready for these spiritual attacks, yet many were not. It is not surprising that as soon as Jesus was baptized and the Spirit of God descended on Him, He was led to the desert before his earthly ministry. In that place, our enemy tempted Jesus.

Jesus was tempted by the devil to abandon the difficult road ahead and take the shortcut to power, wealth and glory. The devil wanted to stop Jesus from fulfilling God's plan and sought to separate Him from God's purpose - the same tactic he used in the garden with Adam and Eve. This should be a clue for us to recognize some of his tactics that we will address in the next chapter.

"If you are the Son of God, tell these stones to become bread." Luke 4:3 (NIV)

With the first temptation, the devil started by questioning Jesus' divinity, challenging Him to prove His power by satisfying His hunger. After forty days without food, Jesus was famished and the devil tempted Jesus with the first thing on Jesus' mind: Food. Even in weakness and intense hunger, Jesus' words said that He would not live for His own appetites but would live to follow God's will; God comes first. Jesus responded:

> *"It is written: 'Man shall not live on bread alone."* Luke 4:4 (NIV)

The enemy then took Jesus to the top of a mountain and showed Him the entire kingdom of Earth. This temptation was the biggest of all. The offer: to be like God. The sin that caused Satan to fall in the first place.

> *And he said to him, "I will give you all their authority and splendor; it has been given to me, and I can give it to anyone I want to. If you worship me, it will all be yours."* Luke 4:5-7 (NIV)

Jesus responded:

> *"It is written: 'Worship the Lord your God and serve him only.'* Luke 4:8 (NIV)

The enemy then took Jesus to the top of the Temple of Jerusalem and quoted Psalm 91:11-12 challenging Him again to prove His divinity and test God by jumping from the temple.

> *"If you are the Son of God," he said, "throw yourself down. For it is written: 'He will command His angels concerning you, and they will lift you up in their hands, so that you will not strike your foot against a stone.'"*
> Luke 4:9-11 (NIV)

Yes, the devil quoted Scripture. But the devil twisted the meaning of the Scripture, a tactic he still uses today. He was trying to get Jesus to misuse the true intention of the Scripture. The Psalms speak of God's protection to those who trust Him, but the promise is not to be used as a way of testing God. But Jesus understood that He was to serve God only. Not vice versa. It all goes back to the will of God. It is not about what we want, but what God wants. Jesus responded:

> *'Do not put the Lord your God to the test.'* Luke 4:12 (NIV)

So we see that Jesus' temptations follow three tactics that our enemy continues to use today. The first temptation concerns the lust of the flesh. The second temptation concerns the pride of life. The third temptation concerns the lust of the eyes

Jesus faced the enemy head on, in his weakest human state, and emerged victorious. He was even more victorious on the cross, but in both of these areas we will leave to later a discussion in this book. However, the war was just beginning between Jesus and the enemy. During His earthly ministry, Jesus cast out demons from various people on numerous occasions. These instances, of course, affirmed His belief in their real existence.

In Matthew 12:22-29, we see Jesus commanding a demon to leave a blind and mute man, and the man was able to speak and see as a result. Jesus' action challenged and shook the religious leaders of that day. Expelling demons from people was not uncommon for the Jewish culture. However, they didn't understand how a simple carpenter had the authority He demonstrated.

In Matthew 15:22-28, we find a Canaanite woman who had a daughter who was severely oppressed by a demon. After seeing her faith, Jesus declared her daughter healed and it happened instantly. Later in Matthew 17:14-20, a man brought his epileptic son for healing. Jesus' disciples couldn't cast out the demon, but Jesus was able. Afterwards, He taught them that it required more faith than they apparently had to cast out that kind of a demon.

Mark describes an interesting observation in Mark 5:1-16. A man possessed with a "legion" of demons. When they, the demons, saw Jesus, they were immediately afraid. They were acutely aware of who Jesus was and the authority and power given to Him by God. After the demon-possessed man had been healed, those who had known him previously saw the miraculous change in him.

Rebuking the enemy in many cases lead to healing, though that was not always the case. Jesus' ministry was focused on "setting the captives free". This consisted of physical and mental healing, rebuking possession and oppression of the enemy, and bringing people back to a right relationship with God. He also passed on this knowledge to His disciples as the foundation to a life of victory.

Cultural reality

We see in the Scripture, who Satan is and how he came to be the devil. We see that he is the leader of a host of angels and demons that joined him in his revolt against God - all of whom were expelled from heaven and the very presence of God.

We see him showing up in the life and ministry of Jesus Christ and, of course, we see Jesus defeating Satan with regards to temptation. We also see Jesus dealing with demons, expelling them from people that they inhabited and oppressed with all kinds of maladies and evils. Jesus defeated Satan all the way from the beginning of His ministry to the end.

In all of this biblical reality, we can conclude that the enemy is real and that he is at his work opposing the purpose and counsel of Christ in the universe. Now we want to see if after the death and resurrection of Jesus Christ from the dead, which was his ultimate defeat, whether he still continued to execute his mission of opposing the course of Christ and His kingdom.

Satan Persecutes the Church

Satan's work of opposing the cause of Christ and of His kingdom continued still even in the church. In Revelation 12:13, we see Satan come against the church, wherein the woman mentioned here is thought to be symbolic of the church. *"And when the dragon saw that he had been thrown down to the earth, he pursued the woman who had given birth to the male child."*

Again in Revelation 12:10 and 13:2-7, we see another picture of satanic persecution of the church, wherein the dragon referred to in the passages is thought to be symbolic of the world's persecution, empowered by Satan, of the church[2].

SATAN SEEKS TO OPPOSES THE GOSPEL

Again, we see Satan in the course of Christianity not only persecuting the church but also actually opposing the Gospel. The apostle describes it this way in 2 Corinthians 4:4 (NIV): *"The god of this age has blinded the minds of unbelievers, so that they cannot see the light of the gospel of the glory of Christ, who is the image of God."*

The Gospel of Matthew puts it this way: *"When anyone hears the message about the kingdom and does not understand it, the evil one comes and snatches away what was sown in their heart. This is the seed sown along the path"* Matthew 13:19 (NIV). The writer of the Gospel of Mark added clearly that when someone hears the gospel, *"Satan comes and takes away the word that was sown in them."* Mark 4:15 (NIV).

In Luke 8:12 (NIV) reads: *"Those along the path are the ones who hear, and then the devil comes and takes away the word from their hearts, so that they may not believe and be saved."* This clearly shows how active the enemy is in preventing the Good News from being accepted by those who need to hear its life-giving message.

The Scripture also says in Matthew 13:38-39 (NIV) that, *"The field is the world, and the good seed stands for the people of the kingdom. The weeds are the people of the evil one, and the enemy who sows them is the devil. The harvest is the end of the age, and the harvesters are angels."*

In this passage we see another sort of satanic opposition of the gospel. The enemy has people, men and woman, to whom he has assigned the responsibility to ensure that is gospel is opposed at all cost. We see a sorcerer by the name Elymas acting on behalf of the devil in Acts chapter 13: *"But Elymas the sorcerer (for that is what his name means) opposed them and tried to turn the proconsul from the faith."* Acts 13:8 (NIV). Satan has not changed.

In 1Thessalonians 2:2, 18 (NIV), Paul tells of his own experience with a satanic opposition of the gospel in his own ministry. *"We had previously suffered and been treated outrageously in Philippi, as you know, but with the help of our God we dared to tell you his gospel in the face of strong opposition . . . For we wanted to come to you—certainly I, Paul, did, again and again—but Satan blocked our way."*

SINFUL HUMAN NATURE IS AN ENEMY

Another tool the devil uses apart from demon spirits is the human flesh. The Bible has many names for the flesh. It is called the "old man", "the carnal man", and "the senses" but they all mean the same thing. The point is if the physical body is not given to God and yielded to the Holy Spirit completely, it is a tool in the hand of the devil.

The Scripture in Galatians 5:17 (NIV) says; *"For the flesh desires what is contrary to the Spirit, and the Spirit what is contrary to the flesh. They are in conflict with each other, so that you are not to do whatever you want."*

Moreover, in 1 Peter 2:11 (NIV), the apostle Peter warns the believer of the impending danger that Satan through the flesh can constitute: *"Dear friends, I urge you, as foreigners and exiles, to abstain from sinful desires, which wage war against your soul."* Sinful desires of the flesh fight against the soul or spirit which simply means the devil can employ our flesh to destroy the believer. Similarly, Paul, therefore, urges the believer not to let sin reign in his mortal body that he obeys its evil desires. (Romans 6:12)

In his intent to making Christians sin against God, Satan seeks to trip us by way of temptation. This is why Paul says in 1Thessalonians 3:5 (NIV): *"For this reason, when I could stand it no longer, I sent to find out about your faith. I was afraid that in some way the tempter had tempted you and that our labors might have been in vain."* Satan is always tempting believers and will continue to do so.

We see first and foremost how he tempted Jesus. And it would be well for us to know that if he tempted Jesus, he would also tempt you and me.

"Because he himself suffered when he was tempted, he is able to help those who are being tempted." Hebrews 2:18 (NIV)

"For we do not have a high priest who is unable to empathize with our weaknesses, but we have one who has been tempted in every way, just as we are—yet he did not sin." Hebrews 4:15 (NIV)

Knowing this should build courage in our hearts to stand up to Satan and resist him when he comes for surely, he will come.

Spiritual warfare

Spiritual warfare has its origin in a rebellion of many angels against God. Satan is seen as the prince of this world, leading an array of forces opposed to God. Although disarmed by Jesus Christ on the cross, Satan and the rebellious angels still remain a powerful threat to the church and to individual believers today[3]. While Satan is still a dangerous enemy even today, Jesus Himself prays for us and has given us the powerful weapons of prayer, faith, and His blood

Hope Is Not Lost

At this point, you might think that all hope is lost. But I want to remind you that in all these things, God is not taken aback for all of this is the outworking of His eternal purpose.

> *"In Him we have obtained an inheritance, having been predestined according to the purpose of Him who works all things according to the counsel of His will."* Ephesians 1:11 (NKJV)

And we know that God is in control of history and has plans for each one of us. In Isaiah 46:9–10 (NKV), the Scripture says: *"Remember the former things of old; for I am God, and there is no other; I am God, and there is none like me, declaring the end from the beginning and from ancient times things not yet done, saying, 'My counsel shall stand, and I will accomplish all my purpose."*

Again, the Scripture says: *"Therefore do not be foolish, but understand what the will of the Lord is."* Ephesians 5:17

We need to understand that God is sovereign. He is bigger than the devil. However, some Christians have a greater fear of the devil than they have of God. At the end of the day we really have nothing to fear.

> *'You, dear children, are from God and have overcome them, because the one who is in you is greater than the one who is in the world.'* 1 John 4:4 (NIV)

It is this attitude that we should embrace the life in Christ.

Jesus paid the price for our freedom and wants to give us abundant life, and that includes shattering the strongholds that hold us captive. However, we need to know that this life includes a good warfare. We must fight the good fight of faith. This is a battle fought in the spiritual realm.

> *"For though we live in the world, we do not wage war as the world."* 2 Corinthians.10:3 (NIV)

> *"Timothy, my son, I am giving you this command in keeping with the prophecies once made about you, so that by recalling them you may fight the*

battle well, holding on to faith and a good conscience, which some have rejected and so have suffered shipwreck with regard to the faith." 1 Timothy 1:18-19 (NIV)

"Fight the good fight of the faith. Take hold of the eternal life to which you were called when you made your good confession in the presence of many witnesses." 1 Timothy 6:12 (NIV)

I wonder how many of you will not fight when you know that the fight you are in is a good one and that the end is already determined? VICTORY!

AGAINST THE DEVIL

Our fight is not against human beings, but it is against the enemy himself. The promise of this fight was given us in the Scripture at the very dawn of creation at the fall of Adam and Eve. *"And I will put enmity between you and the woman, and between your offspring and hers; he will crush your head, and you will strike his heel"* Genesis 3:15 (NIV).

The writers of the New Testament made it even more direct and more specific. The apostle Paul said, *"For our struggle is not against flesh and blood, but against the rulers, against the authorities, against the powers of this dark world and against the spiritual forces of evil in the heavenly realms"* Ephesians 6:12 (NIV).

The apostle James in James 4:7 (NIV) takes it a little further when he said: *"Submit yourselves, then, to God. Resist the devil, and he will flee from you."* We are directed to resist the enemy. The apostle Peter said, *"Be alert and of sober mind. Your enemy the devil prowls around like a roaring lion looking for someone to devour"* 1 Peter. 5:8 (NIV).

Finally, the apostle John in the Revelation reported that the fight, even at the end of the age, will be with Satan. *"Then the dragon was enraged at the woman and went off to wage war against the rest of her offspring—those who keep*

God's commands and hold fast their testimony about Jesus" Revelation 12:17 (NIV). The believer's wrestling match is against the enemy and will continue to be so until Satan is finally banished from the earth by God and locked up in the dungeon of the lake of fire forever.

AGAINST THE FLESH

It is important that we know that our struggle and fight are with the enemy. However, most of the time the struggle and fight are also with the flesh, i.e., "the old man" and sinful carnal nature because Satan employs them to work against us.

The apostle Paul spoke of his struggle against this sinful nature in the following words: *"But I see another law at work in me, waging war against the law of my mind and making me a prisoner of the law of sin at work within me"* Romans 7:23 (NIV). In another passage, he said: *"Everyone who competes in the games goes into strict training. They do it to get a crown that will not last, but we do it to get a crown that will last forever. Therefore I do not run like someone running aimlessly; I do not fight like a boxer beating the air. No, I strike a blow to my body and make it my slave so that after I have preached to others, I myself will not be disqualified for the prize"* 1 Corinthians 9:25–27 (NIV). He knew that his body (flesh) and soul (mind, will, and emotions) were a problem and that they had to be put under check otherwise Satan would utilize them against him.

You and I are not strangers to the fight between our flesh and the Spirit. There have been many times has your body told you not to do what the Spirit through the Word told you to do. The apostle Paul, having had his own share of the struggle between his flesh and the Holy Spirit, summarized it thus: *"For the flesh desires what is contrary to the Spirit, and the Spirit what is contrary to the flesh. They are in conflict with each other, so that you are not to do whatever you want"* Galatians 5:17 (NIV).

Peter gave us the effect of fleshly desires. He said: *"Dear friends, I urge you, as foreigners and exiles, to abstain from sinful desires, which wage war against your soul"* 1 Peter. 2:11 (NIV). The soul is the target of this war, and we know that when the soul is down, the man is down.

Given this, we must never forget that we have been given a preview of Satan's final downfall when we read the last page of God's history! For we know the prophetic Word says: *"And the devil who had deceived them was thrown into the lake of fire and sulfur where the beast and the false prophet were, and they will be tormented day and night forever and ever"* Revelation 20:10 (NIV). That is his determined and sure end. We do not have to be afraid.

You may have heard this saying: "When Satan reminds you of your past, remind him of his future." That's it! His future is the lake of fire and sulfur where he will be tormented forever and ever. Therefore, cheer up: you have overcome.

The Kingdom Of Heaven

Understanding who Satan is and his main purpose of opposing Christ, His purpose and His kingdom on earth, we must, as believers, answer the call by God as His special agents to advance His kingdom against the resistance of this enemy-Satan.

God depends on us to advance His kingdom, and he has furnished us for the battle. We must come to the understanding that *"the Kingdom of Heaven has been forcefully advancing, and violent people are attacking it"* (Mt 11:12 NLT).

You may be asking; what is the kingdom? The kingdom is the realm where Jesus rules, where His word is obeyed. Better still, the kingdom of God is the sphere of God's influence, where His power and glory prevails, where His word reigns and rules, and where the influence of God's Spirit's prevails and permeates.

As wonderful as the kingdom may seem, because of the opposition of Satan, it requires a forceful attitude to obtain all the kingdom has to offer

– all its glory and beauties engrafted in God's Word of promise. It takes doggedness, hardness and toughness to advance God's interests on the earth while standing and pushing against real satanic opposition. This is because every advancement of the purpose of God will be greeted with resistance from spiritual powers from hell. This means that we have to be strong and take on the full armor of God to do battle in the kingdom and bring to bear on the earth His purposes against all resistance whatsoever.

That being said, I firmly believe that we are living in an appointed time, a period in history and in our individual life that is demanding the Church body to rise up and stand against the enemy by every means possible according to the Word of God.

If we look at what is happening in our world today, in our culture, and in our society, we can see the enemy's hand at work. But I think that many believers who are sensitive to the Holy Spirit have recognized this and have begun to cooperate with God and His timing. We know that our God is a God of order, not of chaos. So where there is hate, we must respond in love. Where there is war, we must respond in peace. *"There is a time for everything, and a season for every activity under the heavens"* Ecclesiastes 3:1 (NIV).

So then: *"Whoever obeys his command will come to no harm, and the wise heart will know the proper time and procedure. For there is a proper time and procedure for every matter, though a person may be weighed down by misery"* Ecclesiastes 8:5-6 (NIV).

So are you are going to obey God's command to stand up against the enemy? God is counting on you and there no harm to those who do as guaranteed by the Scripture.

CHAPTER THREE - BATTLEFIELD

The reason why many fail in the battle is because they wait until the hour of battle. The reason why others succeed is because they have gained their victory on their knees long before the battle came.
R. A. TORREY

I remember waking up suddenly at two o'clock in the morning. My wife was sound asleep in bed beside me. But something else was in the room, and I will never forget what happened over the next few minutes. I was in a struggle, a wrestling match with some demonic force. At the time, I had no clue what was going on. It was a full on struggle. I was pushing back against this force, grunting, sweating, trying to move and gain the upper hand. However, I was losing the battle. There was no reprieve and I finally just gave up. At that moment, it all stopped and went away. Or so I thought. Whatever demonic spirit I had battled had taken hold, and I gave it permission to have control over a part of my life. I had no clue what it was so I never told my wife what happened until years later.

I didn't know all this at the time. Unfortunately, while some believers may not have gone through this type of experience, they have given the right to the enemy to set up camp in their lives and give control to him. We are in the midst of a spiritual conflict. Ephesians 6:12 (NIV) states: *"for our struggle is not against flesh and blood, but against the rulers, against the authorities, against the powers of this dark world and against the spiritual forces of evil in the heavenly realms."*

That evening, I wasn't wrestling with a physical body, but with a spiritual force of evil in the spiritual realm. I was wide-awake, but could not see what I was fighting. We need to understand that we are in a spiritual battle, and it takes a different set of tactics to engage in it. We do not fight with our power but by the Spirit. If I would have been aware of that fact, I imagine the wrestling match would have ended differently that night. Remember, that the weapons we fight with are not the weapons of the world. Our weapons have divine power to demolish strongholds.

The attack that night was very targeted as well. Somehow, in my limited spiritual knowledge, I knew I was wrestling with a demonic spirit associated with lust. That was my weak area, even as a married Christian man. The demonic spirit wanted to keep me from stepping into my purpose and the plan God created for me and kept me a weak introverted man. This evil spirit was waging a war in my mind and made me a prisoner of the sin at work within me.

Just a few months ago as I was reading 1 Peter 4, I across a passage that instantly took me back to that experience. *"Dear friends, do not be surprised at the fiery ordeal that has come on you to test you, as though something strange were happening to you"* 1 Peter 4:12 (NIV). It felt like an ordeal. It was strenuous, a struggle, and it was very frightening. And it didn't just end that evening. The struggle with that sin was continuous. It lasted years, and it got worse. So much that it almost caused me to lose my marriage.

The Battlefield

The battle has waged in the spiritual realm and the physical realm since creation. Spiritual warfare is the struggle of evil forces in our minds. The Bible states that this battle is fought not on a physical plane at all, but a spiritual one. This might be all new to you. I didn't have the revelation that there was complete freedom from sin, or how to oppose the enemy when he attacked or how to resist, overcome, and defeat the enemy when he attacked.

Maybe you are like me and gave room to allow the enemy to operate. It's a choice. We open the door. We take of the apple.

Maybe you have allowed your mind to believe the deceptive lies of the enemy. You may not have realized the cause of lie, but you feel like you are going around and around a mountain. You are stuck in a pattern of sin, failure, and immaturity. You believe Satan's lies, and are unable to change and are caught in a repetitive habitual sin. You feel immature in your faith, not knowing how to remove this pattern of sin and defeat the enemy.

The thing about our enemy is that he will start with something small. Getting you to think about something. Deceiving you into thinking that it is okay. You justify it in your head. You willingly co-operate with the enemy. From there, you act upon that thought. Over time, it becomes a habit. Then it forms who you are, your character. Ultimately it becomes your lifestyle unless you stop it at the beginning.

What starts off as a simple glance at an inappropriate ad on the Internet can lead, unchecked, to a full-blown addiction to pornography. It may not happen overnight, but the enemy will get you thinking about the ad over and over. He will convince you to justify your thoughts even before you act. You then start hiding things, deleting your browsing history, viewing sites on work computers, etc. With each action, you are building a supporting stronghold, each one reinforcing the initial lie you believed from the devil.

Over time, there is an impact on your life. You start to oppose the knowledge of God. The intimacy and relationship you once had with Him are now gone. You start to oppose the purpose He has for your life. The destiny He has for you is clouded and you can't see what lies ahead. You unknowingly limit the potential of what you could be and could do. Your mind, instead, is filled with lies and deception, and pretty soon, you just accept that this is your "sinful nature", and it controls your life.

There is a promise in God's Word: *"You will know the truth, and the truth will set you free"* John 8:32 (NIV). There is, however, a way through this endless cycle of sin. You may be looking out on the battlefield, and everything is hopeless. But you have a truth that you need to understand and hold on to. If we look back into the Old Testament, we see that God gave the nation of Israel a divine revelation on how to conquer the enemies they faced in the Promised Land.

The key to victory for the nation of Israel was their understanding that the Lord would deliver all of their enemies into their hands (Deuteronomy 2:36). All things are possible to him that believes. God worked with the Israelites and on their behalf to ensure victory. We have the same Lord working for our freedom. In fact, we have a Savior, who gave His life on the cross for us to become conquerors. Be strong and courageous and step out onto the battlefields. Learn about how our enemy engages to rebuke his actions.

From the previous chapter, you can see the variety of names Satan has that gives us hints about the multiple ways he can attack us. From being described as a dragon in Revelation, to an "angel of light" in 2 Corinthians, Satan adapts to situations and uses a variety of tactics to take our focus off God and onto ourselves. While Satan is not omniscient, he has had all of human history to study us and observe the best way to deceive us. He has learned with astonishing accuracy what will best tempt and defeat us.

There are multiple areas, or battlefields, that Satan can attack us on.

ATTACKS AGAINST GOD

A counterfeit is "an imitation intended to be passed off fraudulently or deceptively as genuine[1]". This is the main area of battle that Satan uses concerning God. Satan desired to be like God. That was his original sin, trying to provide a counterfeit kingdom. In Genesis 3:5, Satan presented this counterfeit kingdom when he told Eve that she and Adam would "be like God, knowing good and evil." He did the same with Jesus when he tempted Him in the desert. Satan was trying to show Jesus a way of having the glory that was rightfully His, but without the critical piece of His death on the cross.

Today, Satan promotes a form of godliness while denying its power (2 Timothy 3:5). We have many churches preaching about walking with God, but they leave out the "power" aspect.

The apostle Paul warned against Satan *"masquerading as an angel of light"*, and his servants (evil spirits) *"masquerade as servants of righteousness."* He warned Timothy that people would abandon the faith and follow deceiving spirits taught by demons. They would create a false doctrinal system that is focused away from God and to self-serving methods. While these teachers may look and seem "Christian", the people needed to look and evaluate their fruit to determine if they are counterfeit.

Demons, evil or unclean spirits, act as Satan's emissaries to promote his purpose of thwarting the plan of God. Satan experiences creaturely limitations, but demons extend his power and activities significantly. In fact, at times it may seem that Satan enjoys omniscience and omnipresence, however, in actuality he does not. It is just that the demons extend Satan's activities so much that one might think Satan himself is doing it all. Having chosen to rebel against God and side with Satan, demons continue to oppose the purposes of God in this world.

On occasion, God may use demons to further His purposes. He sent an evil spirit to stir up the people of Shechem against Abimelech (Judges 9:23). He used an evil spirit to torment Saul with a mental disturbance that bordered on madness (1 Samuel 16:14-15). He sent a deceiving spirit to control the prophets and to give Ahab the wrong advice (2 Chronicles 18:21). Because they are creatures, demons are accountable to God and thus can be used by Him to bring His people back into right relationship with Him.

ATTACKS AGAINST JESUS CHRIST

The battlefield between Satan and Christ started after the sin of Adam and Eve (Genesis 3:15). Enmity was put between Satan and God's creation. God said an individual from among the "woman's seed" would deal a fatal blow to Satan's head while Satan would bruise the heel of the woman's seed. The climax of this battle took place on the cross.

When Jesus came to this earth in human form, Satan made concerted attempts to thwart His purpose to die for the sins of the world. The harsh reaction that Herod had when learning he was tricked by the wise men led to a mass killing of the children under two had to be Satan-inspired (Matthew 2:16). Christ even stated that Peter aligned himself with Satan's plan when Peter wanted to reject the idea that Christ would have to die (Matthew 16:21–23). The sharpness of Christ's rebuke stresses the fact that His central purpose in coming to earth was to die. When Judas was about to betray Jesus, Satan entered into him (John 13:27).

But the most direct attack of Satan on our Lord was at His temptation in the desert (Matthew 4:1–11) as we discussed in the previous chapter. Satan was trying to cause our Lord to deviate from the path and purpose for which He came into the world and to make Himself independent from God and His plan by offering Him glory without suffering.

There is no doubt that Satan's believed that Christ is the promised Deliverer. He just did not want that to come fully to pass.

Satan had been given authority over this world, temporarily, but Christ will ultimately rule it. Thus, Satan had the right to offer the Lord the kingdoms of this world, but if Christ took Satan's offer, He would have shortcut the plan of God and bypassed the atoning work of His death. Satan tempts us by having us focus on instant gratification, rather than waiting on God's provision.

Since Satan was unsuccessful in preventing the Jesus' death on the cross, he goes after and attacks the Gospel, those who follow Christ, and what the plans of God for this world.

Attack Against The Nations

Satan's major "earthly" battlefield is the nations. Revelation 20:3 states that he *"deceives the nations."* We see this time and time again throughout history with leaders and kings. Satan convinces them that they can govern righteously and attempt to bring peace. All this while being apart from the presence and rule of Christ. Satan's tactic of deception is at work among these leaders and kings.

Satan utilizes all aspects of his army in carrying out his deception. Daniel's answer to prayer in form of an angel was hindered due to a powerful demonic force in Persia. Satan also uses governments to hinder the progress of the Gospel (1 Thessalonians 2:18). Paul attempted to come to the Thessalonian church but was hindered by Satan.

We turn on the news and see the turmoil and wars in the Middle East, contests over the nation of Israel, God's chosen people. There has never been another country so heavily attacked and fought over as the nation of Israel.

In carrying out their opposition to God, demons actively try to turn men to the worship of idols. This was true in Old Testament times and is widespread in the nations, both near and far today. Our family loves to travel, and there are few countries that we have visited where we can see and feel the enemy at work in their culture.

Attacks Against Unbelievers

We also see Satan blinding the minds of unbelievers so that they will not accept the Gospel (2 Corinthians 4:4). He deceives unbelievers by making them think that ANY way to heaven is as acceptable as the ONLY way, which is through Jesus Christ. The enemy comes and takes away the Word that people have received to prevent them from believing (Luke 8:12).

Our Position on the Battlefield

We will learn quickly how the enemy engages with us specifically on these battlefields. But if you are like me, I needed to know what it takes to face the enemy.

The battle we must engage in is spiritual, individual, hard and persistent. It calls for courage, perseverance, and prayer. Believers must rely upon God's strength and utilize the armor He has provided.

We must engage the enemy. We are on the battlefield in our church, in our work, in our homes, and in our marriages. We are not warring against other people, but with the enemy who is utilizing each battlefield to his advantage. We have the authority to take over that battlefield.

In Deuteronomy 2:24, the Lord stated: *"Rise up, set out on your journey and go over the Valley of the Arnon. Behold, I have given into your hand Sihon the Amorite, king of Heshbon, and his land. Begin to take possession, and contend with him in battle"*

If we adopt the attitude of victory that God gave the nation of Israel as it made their way to the Promised Land, we will start to walk in victory. *"I have given into your hand ... begin to possess it, contend with him in the battle."* The promise of victory was assured. We must believe God that our victory is secured on the battlefield. We too "have been given" victory.

Sihon, in Deuteronomy 2:24, represents the demonic realm that resists and opposes advancement. From scripture we see that Sihon had a stubborn spirit and refused to grant Israel passage, thus opposing the progression of God's people. We see the same stubbornness and opposition in the spiritual realm. Our enemies are unseen spiritual forces that operate from the spiritual world. Our battle is not with people, flesh and blood, but spiritual forces. We must recognize the nature of the conflict and understand how to win.

We need to "rise up" and "take our journey". Can't you just envision one of the massive epic battles portrayed by Hollywood when the leader of the vast army rallies his troops and encourages them as they go into battle? "RISE UP," he yells. This stirs something in the men. It is a call to arms, a decree to stand up and fight in the midst of potential demise. Something clicks in their mind, and the men have a new mental attitude towards the battle. What looked hopeless is transformed into a renewed hope for victory.

But it is more than just to rise up or stand. We must move. We need to "take journey". In this context, the nation of Israel was living out of tents as they travelled. Thus, "take journey" means to pull the tent pins, to prepare oneself for change by pulling out everything that was locked into place. The same is true in our lives. We must remove and get rid of anything that is locking us into a position on the battlefield that is leaving us stuck on the sidelines and getting killed by collateral damage.

Victory Assured

Victory is guaranteed if we engage in the battle. We must "begin to possess it". There was a promise in that statement. Start the work, and He will complete it. Possess means to take occupation, to have ownership of someplace that was previously inhabited. Whatever has ruled your life, you must take dominion and dispossess what the enemy has taken.

Now, with this promised possession, there is a confrontation. There is a battle, an engagement of the enemy face to face, a conflict to prevail over. There is no quick fix to long-standing personal issues. We have to engage with a long-term victory with occupation in mind.

Rest assured that as you read this book, you will receive an outline and more insight and revelation into how to rise up on the battlefield and emerge victorious. For now, rest in the promise that God gave the nation of Israel seen in Deuteronomy 2:36 *"There was not a city to high for us. The LORD our God gave all into our hands."* Victory is secured; there is no one too strong for you through Him.

As we engage the enemy on the battlefields, we need to know the specific tactics he uses in battle, and how to overcome them.

CHAPTER FOUR - ENEMY TACTICS

"Two are better than one because they have a good reward for their labor. For if they fall, one will lift up his companion. But woe to him who is alone when he falls, for he has no one to help him up. Again, if two lie down together, they will keep warm; but how can one be warm alone? Though one may be overpowered by another, two can withstand him. And a threefold cord cannot be broken." Ecclesiastes 4:9-12 (NKJV)

Ecclesiastes 4:9 states that there is strength in numbers when we stand together. However, the opposite is also true. We experience more problems when we are isolated and go it alone. Trying to "manage" sin by yourself does not lead to victory. It isolates you in your relationships. Proverbs 18:1 (NKJV) states: *"a man who isolates himself seeks his own desire; he rages against all wise judgment."*

We see a prime example of this when Elijah faced spiritual pressure from Satan and his enemy in 1 Kings 19. Elijah was a prophet and poised to transform the nation. God had worked major supernatural miracles through Elijah. There had been a spiritual and relational drought, primarily brought about Jezebel, who controlled the king. She ruled and influenced the nation, using King Ahab to do the work, directed by her. Being influenced by demonic forces, she attacked and killed God's prophets and replaced them with her own who were loyal to Baal, a false god at that time in that region. As you will recall from the previous chapter, Satan, and his demons often posed as other gods and influenced people into oppression.

Elijah confronted these prophets of Baal and killed them. Obviously, the confrontation did not sit well with Jezebel as she reacted against him and sent a messenger to Elijah stating that if he continued doing what he is doing, he would not live to see tomorrow.

While we may not have received a verbal death threat from someone who has a vendetta against us, the enemy does speak death to us if we let him. Evil messages come in many forms: criticism, threats, manipulation, and curses. In some cases, behind the message or the messenger is an evil spirit whose goal is to remove you from your position of influence in Christ.

Fear, indecisiveness, discouragement, confusion, loneliness, despair feeling overwhelmed. These emotions flooded Elijah as part of the spiritual attack. He was fearful of death, so he yielded to the attack and shut down. In 1 Kings 19:3, it states that he *"ran for his life."* He focused on self-preservation and withdrew from the challenge. He tried to avoid the issue but, more importantly, he withdrew from the assignment that God had given.

He took himself out of relationship with those who had stood behind him. He isolated himself when he *"left his servant"*. He *"sat down"* and in his isolation and passivity, he was overcome by rejection, despair, and hopelessness. He desired to die. Satan's spiritual attack through Jezebel was successful as it caused Elijah to yield in fear and isolated himself instead of rising to the challenge. He lost all perspective of what God had done for, and through, him, and stated, *"I alone am left."*

YOU ARE NOT ALONE

Maybe you feel like this sometimes. You feel alone and isolated. Your sin is shameful, and the enemy keeps reminding you of what you did and calls into question your salvation.

Christians are at war with their flesh, this world, and the enemy. Externally, Satan utilizes the things of this world to attack believers, persecuting, deceiving and seducing them. Internally, believers strive to serve God, yet sinfulness frustrates their efforts. There are three major ways that we can expect the enemy to attack. We must learn how the enemy uses these tactics and how we can defend against them so we can walk in a life of victory.

FIERY DARTS

Spiritual warfare is resisting, overcoming and defeating the lies, temptations and accusations the enemy sends our way. We need to be both offensive and defensive to adequately live in victory

Offensive warfare is tearing down the strongholds the enemy has formed in our mind through deception and accusations, whereas defensive warfare is guarding ourselves against the tactics or schemes of the devil.

In defensive spiritual warfare, Satan's commands demonic spirits to launch *"fiery darts"* against us. Ephesians 6:16 (KJV) states: *"Above all, taking the shield of faith, wherewith ye shall be able to quench all the fiery darts of the wicked."*

Unfortunately many translations of the Bible use the term "darts" or "arrows" when describing the attack of our enemy. We may immediately think of a little bullseye dart and believe that we will experience a little innocent attack. However, the word "dart" in this scripture comes from the Greek word *belos*, which means a javelin, or missile[1]. Rest assured; Satan is not throwing small little arrows at us. These are not annoying little darts that we can swat away. These are long thick arrows, the length of a javelin, which was commonly shot out of war machine or catapult.

These "fiery darts" are temptations, deceptions, and accusations.

DECEPTION

When you deceive someone, you attempt to make that person believe a lie or something that is not true. When the enemy uses deception, it is an attempt to deceive you into believing something that is not true to cause you to fall into sin.

In the beginning, Satan deceived Eve into believing that God's Word was not true. Genesis 3:4, states that the devil told her *"you will not surely die"* which contradicts what God said stated in Genesis 2:17.

The serpent's first tactic, deception, caused doubt in the mind of the woman. He asked some questions to twisted what she "thought" she heard and thus, misrepresented the truth. The enemy questioned Eve's understanding with the subtle additional query, *"Did He really say?"* This was the first deception. It took Eve away from God's Word and into her own mind and thoughts to try to determine what God said.

While subtle, Satan used the name "God" rather than His true covenant name, LORD. He was questioning Eve's understanding of lordship and trying to present God as someone lesser than the LORD of ALL. He cleverly reworked God's commands by slightly changing and omitting words, again causing confusion and doubt. Satan rephrased God's command and fashioned it for his own interests to deceive Eve.

Second Corinthians 11:3 captures what happened, and we need to take heed of the warning: *"But I am afraid that as the serpent deceived Eve by his cunning, your thoughts will be led astray from a sincere and pure devotion to Christ."* (ESV)

I see the enemy knock down great men and women of God. It makes my blood boil when I see Christians serving God and living out the destiny and plan He created, only to fall to a mere lie that the enemy planted. They end up living in defeat because they were deceived. I was one of them! The enemy deceives us and causes us to believe and live out a lie.

When we allow a deception to take hold, a stronghold forms in our mind. Strongholds are incorrect thinking patterns based on a lie. Demonic spirits love to use these strongholds to their advantage. These strongholds have tremendous power to affect our feelings and emotions. Many believers still feel guilt-ridden and worthless because they don't see themselves the way they should, even though they have committed their life to Christ. Many Christians feel unloved and not good enough to be accepted by God because they see Him in a wrong way. Their perception of Him is tainted, and it causes them to see Him as an indirect and harsh overseer instead of a close, loving Father who sincerely desires to have an intimate, loving relationship with them! This stronghold is an incorrect thinking pattern that stems from believing something that is not true.

We have two weapons to deal with deception: the belt of truth (Ephesians 6:14) and the sword of the Spirit (Ephesians 6:17) both of which are the Word of God. The Word of God is the truth. Thus, the *"belt"* in this scripture is meant to be defensive; the *"sword"* is meant to be offensive. The Word of God is an offensive and defensive weapon.

Use both the belt of truth and the sword of the Spirit, to guard against deceptions the enemy uses. Use God's Word to tear down existing strongholds, or deceptions; that took hold in your mind.

In Romans 12:2 (KJV), we are told to *"be not conformed to this world: but be ye transformed by the renewing of your mind."* We can renew our minds by reading and studying God's Word, so we know the difference between the Truth of God and the lies of Satan. In Ephesians 5:26 (KJV), this process is referred to as washing of water by the Word: *"That he might sanctify and cleanse it with the washing of water by the word."*

TEMPTATION

Temptation often follows deception. Temptation occurs when we are enticed or encouraged to sin. The enemy first tells us, *"You won't surely die!"* Then he makes sin, the fruit of the forbidden tree, look good to us. Eve believed Satan's deception that the tree she was not supposed to eat from looked good to her. She was tempted, or enticed, to sin, because she allowed herself to be deceived.

In Matthew 4, Jesus was led out into the desert to be tempted by the devil. Satan attempted to convince Jesus that it would be harmless to jump off the temple. This is related to when people are drawn to premarital sex with their mate as the enemy convinces them that it is safe and fun. An open door is given to the enemy to walk in and create a stronghold.

Jesus saw through Satan's deception and resisted temptation by speaking God's Word. In Psalms 119:11 (KJV), King David said: *"Thy word have I hid in mine heart, that I might not sin against thee."*

When the enemy is tempting us, he is showing us the worm but behind it is a hook. The Word of God helps you see through his entire deception.

Satan tempts believers in at least three areas. The first is conforming to the pressures of society and culture (1 Thessalonians 3:5). Paul was forced to leave Thessalonica after one month of ministry in that city (Acts

17:5–10). Satan used a government ban to keep Paul from returning (1 Thessalonians. 2:18).

So Paul sent Timothy, who was not under that ban, back to Thessalonica to see if the people had succumbed to Satan's temptations. Satan could have tempted them to continue to conform back to the lifestyles they were accustom to before they became followers of Christ.

The second area Satan tempts believers in is to cover up selfishness. Ananias and Sapphira wanted to preserve some of the money they earned from the sale of their property. They also wanted to receive praise for their contribution. Peter discerned that it was a temptation placed by the enemy which caused them to lie (Acts 5:1–11).

They had every right to own and sell property. They also had no obligation to give all the profit of the sale to the church. But they were obliged not to pretend to give generously while at the same time add to their selfishness by keeping part of the profit.

The third area Satan tempts believers is in respect to immorality (1 Corinthians. 7:5). God created marriage as a proper expression of physical needs and closeness. He expects husbands and wives to understand their individual and mutual responsibilities. Satan can tempt believers to perform illicit or perverted sexual sins when they take their focus off of their covenant made before God.

Satan couldn't damage Eve's relationship with God because he had no rights to her. Instead, he decided to make her give him those rights. He tempted her to sin and sin gives the enemy a legal right to operate in our lives. Ephesians 4:22 tells us to *"put off our old sinful nature."* In verse 27, it states that if we don't, we allow the enemy to create a stronghold in our lives through sin.

Ephesians 4:27 says *"give no opportunity to the devil."* Satan had to tempt Eve in the garden to cause her to sin because he had no 'place' in Eve's life. To break the relationship between Eve and God, he had to create an opportunity for her to sin. If the enemy wants a legal right to your life, he will send temptations your way. That is his method of getting you to fall and give him a place to operate. The moment you fail and sin, it is important to turn quickly from those sins and repent so that you can be forgiven and the legal ground the enemy obtained is returned.

In James 4:7, we are instructed to *"resist the devil, and he will flee from you."* In the same verse, we are also directed *"to draw near to God."* Dealing with temptation is a dual process of resisting the enemy and drawing near to God. The closer relationship you have with God and the more you become aware of His love, and the less power temptation will have over you.

ACCUSATIONS

The devil is known as the *"accuser of the brethren"* (Revelation 12:10). He takes a believer who has done an embarrassing or gross sin in their past, and continues to rub it in his face and beats him down with guilt and condemnation over the past.

The enemy accuses us by reminding us of our past sins and failures. As we listen to his accusations against us, we begin to meditate on our pasts. It is not long after we start to feel guilt-ridden and see ourselves as failures. However, both of these areas were dealt with on the cross! The blood of Jesus has washed away our sin. We must not be thinking about our sins anymore.

Satan loves to take a believer who is washed clean in the blood of Jesus and is without spot or blemish and make him feel dirty, worthless and see himself as a failure. As we pay attention to the enemy's accusations, they form strongholds in our minds that need to be torn away before we can experience freedom.

The fiery darts of the enemy mentioned in Ephesians 6:16 are accusations sent our way. When the enemy attempts to accuse us of our past sins, we are to have faith in the work of the cross. Our sins are forgiven, and we are not to dwell on those past mistakes. Faith is what we use to put out the fiery darts of the enemy (Ephesians 6:16). We are not to focus on our past.

"Stand therefore, having fastened on the belt of truth, and having put on the breastplate of righteousness."
Ephesians 6:14 (ESV)

Our righteous deeds are like *"filthy rags"* (Isaiah 64:6). However, through the work of the cross, we receive the righteousness of God in Christ Jesus (Romans 3:22, Galatians 3:6). When the enemy reminds you of your past, tell him it is wiped away (2 Corinthians 5:17), it is forgotten (Hebrews 10:17) and the righteousness of God is in you (Romans 3:22). Meditate on the Truth, the Word of God!

OUR WEAPONS OF WARFARE

Ephesians 6 lists the weapons at our disposal for spiritual warfare. In Ephesians 6:17 we are told to take up *"...the sword of the Spirit, which is the word of God."*

As mentioned earlier, the sword is the offensive weapon meant to tear down and destroy the enemy. When we meditate on the truth in God's Word, it tears down strongholds. Strongholds are built on false "truths" and are torn down through God's truth.

The enemy might say: "Look at your past! You're a failure!"

God's Word tells you: "The blood of Jesus has washed away my past!"

If you meditate on the error, you feel guilty and see yourself as a failure. When you focus on what God's Word says about you, you begin to feel clean and victorious!

Spiritual warfare is a battle that goes on in our minds between lies and His truth. When we can know the truth and focus on it, while at the same time ignoring the lie, we will be victorious.

THE BATTLE FOR OUR MIND

A stronghold is a deception, an incorrect thinking pattern based on a believed lie that is established in a person's mind. People can get inaccurate perceptions of God by listening to the enemy as he tells them how God doesn't love them, etc. People can feel like dirty sinners when they believe Satan's accusations as he continually reminds them of their past sins which have been washed away.

Strongholds are formed on lies from the enemy. They come in the form of deception or accusations. Accusations lead to guilt and feelings of unworthiness. These weigh you down and tear you apart spiritually.

Since strongholds are created up lies we believe, the way to tear them down strongholds is the truth found in God's Word. It is the opposite of what the enemy has been telling us. If you discover the enemy has been attempting to convince us of a lie, we need to stop believing the enemy and start believing on the word of God.

Strongholds are the enemy's favorite weapon in the battle for our mind, will, and emotions. Take up the sword of the Spirit, God's Word, and start removing the enemy's tactics that he's been using against you!

Let's discover what these common strongholds are and how to tear them down.

CHAPTER FIVE - STRONGHOLDS

As we saw in the previous chapter, the primary battlefield, and tactic the enemy uses, is our mind. While some spiritual attacks can be physical such as unexplained illnesses, etc. the majority of the battles are in our minds. If Satan can get us to think less of ourselves, question the need for our Savior, disobey God's Word, then he has been successful in breaking our relationship with God.

Paul recognized this when he was writing the Corinthian church:

> *"For though we live in the world, we do not wage war as the world does. The weapons we fight with are not the weapons of the world. On the contrary, they have divine power to demolish strongholds. We demolish arguments and every pretension that sets itself up against the knowledge of God, and we take captive every thought to make it obedient to Christ. And we will be ready to punish every act of disobedience, once your obedience is complete."*
> 2 Corinthians 10:3-6 (NIV)

The word stronghold used here comes from the Greek word *ochuroma* that refers to a fortified place inside a walled city. This place was an impregnable fortress. During ancient military times, soldiers would defend from within the stronghold. However, if the stronghold was breached and taken over, the battle was over.

Paul applied this military word in a spiritual sense. He recognized that spiritual warfare most often occurs in the mind, and it has to be subdued and destroyed. He showed that the battle was in our minds when he said that we need to *"take captive every thought."*

Paul is talking about strongholds as mindsets that keep us in bondage. They are incorrect beliefs, thoughts, and knowledge that lead us into to *"acts of disobedience"* (verse 5). The enemy uses lies and deceptions to deceive us into thinking and acting in ways that are contrary to God. At the core, these strongholds come against the true understanding and knowledge of God.

From a psychological standpoint, strongholds could be linked to habitual thinking based on erroneous information that causes us to form bad habits, addictions, and lifestyle choices.

The strongholds that we allow the enemy to establish in us creates hopelessness, leading us to believe something in our lives is unchangeable. Strongholds control our thinking and diminish anything that contradicts it.

As discussed before, the enemy will use lies and deception to obtain a foothold in our life. The biggest lie he wants us to believe is that he is not there, that he is not real. Paul warns us that unbelief in the devil is the devil's work (2 Corinthians 4:4). Satan blinds the minds of those who do not believe from seeing the glory of Christ, and for those who do believe, he blinds them from seeing him.

THE BATTLE IN OUR MIND

A stronghold may seem legitimately real from the outside, but it is chiefly in our perception. The battle is in the mind. If we let the enemy convince us there is no hope, he has already won.

A simple biblical example of this is found in 1 Samuel 17, the classic biblical account of David and Goliath. Goliath was a real "giant". He caused all of Israel to fear, and they felt hopeless in the face of him. No one was willing to step forward and act. They were frozen in fear and remained captive in their thinking.

However, David looked at Goliath as a mere Philistine, who had defied God. To David's brothers, Goliath was a giant nobody could defeat. To David, Goliath was already finished!

> *"You come against me with sword and spear and javelin, but I come against you in the name of the LORD Almighty, the God of the armies of Israel, whom you have defied. This day the LORD will hand you over to me, and I'll strike you down and cut off your head. Today I will give the carcasses of the Philistine army to the birds of the air and the beasts of the earth, and the whole world will know that there is a God in Israel. All those gathered here will know that it is not by sword or spear that the LORD saves; for the battle is the LORD's, and he will give all of you into our hands."*
> 1 Samuel 17:45–47 (NIV)

A stronghold is established when the mind is convinced that the situation is unchangeable and hopeless. Renowned author and speaker, Ed Silvoso provides the most comprehensive and brilliant definition of a spiritual stronghold[1]:

> *"A spiritual stronghold is a mindset impregnated with hopelessness which causes us to accept as unchangeable situations we know are contrary to the will of God."*

To the Israelites, Goliath was a stronghold. To David, the stronghold hardly existed!

To the Israelites, there was no hope. To David, Goliath didn't have a chance!

A stronghold is a mindset where the mind is locked into only one way of seeing something. When we get the knowledge and information to make a decision from the enemy instead of God, we are allowing the enemy to set up a stronghold.

Paul states that we must *"demolish arguments and every pretension that sets itself up against the knowledge of God, and we take captive every thought to make it obedient to Christ."* 2 Corinthians 10:5 (NIV)

There are two words here we need to grasp to ensure we have a complete understanding of what Paul is trying to arm us with. The words are "arguments" and "pretension". Arguments in this context are not petty squabbles between people. The word "argument" here is derived from the Greek word *logismos* which refers to powerful reasoning[2]. The enemy is going to disguise the thoughts as powerful arguments that sound good on the outside, but without you realizing it, contradict God's Word. The enemy isn't shy about doing this either; he is boastful and full of pride. That is why Paul uses the word "pretension". It refers to the pompous reason of the enemy as when Goliath said *"this day I defy the ranks of Israel"* when he was challenging Israel (1 Samuel 17:10).

If we let the stronghold intimidate us, we have already lost the battle. If we see that the battle is the Lord's, and we are not to fear, then victory is assured.

The enemy utilizes a variety of strongholds to put a wedge between God and us. These include both religious strongholds and mental strongholds.

Maybe you have heard false teachings such as those that say God punishes us with sickness or God wants us poor, or piousness equates to prosperity. Or maybe you have heard false doctrines that deny the divinity of Christ or advocate that man is sinless, or salvation is earned. These are strongholds that have been erected, and some church doctrine is built upon them.

Strongholds that are focused on the individual's identity and mind are stubbornness, pride, inferiority/superiority complex, confusion, prejudice, and lying. There is great power in the way we understand things and the way we think. A stronghold is a pattern etched into our minds that cause us to think or perceive things in a certain way.

Our enemy looks for any opportunity to move in where we are vulnerable and exploit the situation. We may say or come into agreement with something that is not of God, and the enemy will use that to establish a foothold. He is constantly looking for ways to take people *"captive to do his will"* (2 Timothy 2:26). Remember, Satan and his followers were once angels. They know God's ways to a greater extent than we do and has an advantage over us in this way.

This may be the first time you have heard the word "stronghold" as it concerns the enemy's strategy over us. Now that you are aware of what they are; you need to learn how to recognize them and identify them. How we cope with a stronghold reveals the strength of our relationship with God regarding lordship. Therefore, this matter touches the heart of our lives. Our enemy does not want us to recognize strongholds, which is all the more reason we must learn more about them.

We must discern and recognize when the enemy is trying to establish a stronghold in our life or discern those that currently exist in our lives so we can tear them down.

While there are many strongholds and ways of categorizing them, I feel that if we understand them in the two following aspects, it will help us more easily address the core root of the stronghold.

False perception of God

When a person sees God incorrectly, has a false understanding of God, they see Him as a cruel, distant and unloving God. Our enemy is against all things of God, including God Himself. What better way to make us feel defeated than to setup lies and deceit about the nature of God? God is a loving Father that desires a relationship with His creation.

I work with many people who state that they feel a distance between them and God. They feel unwanted and unloved by God. They feel like God is mad at them for some reason or another. When a person wonders if God still loves them, it's a good indication that they need to change their perception of God.

There are those who lack the desire for an intimate and close relationship with God. They feel that God is distant and cold, and they do not know an intimate, loving and personal God. They develop irrational fears of God that prevent them from drawing near to Him.

The main reason the world doesn't care about God is that they don't know Him. Maybe you find it hard or boring to spend time with God and would rather do other things. A stronghold may have been created to cause you to have an incorrect perception of Him that needs to be changed. This can lead to a lack of love in a person's heart for God.

There are mental behaviors that can be driven by irrational fears of God. It can drive a person into perfectionism so that God will love and accept them. It can also drive a person to experience obsessive fears of committing what they consider an "unpardonable sin." I have seen many times where a person is harassed by irrational and compulsive blasphemous thoughts against the Holy Spirit, and then self-condemned as being hopeless. It seems the more they fear thinking the thoughts, the worse and more compulsive those thoughts become.

One of the side effects of having an incorrect perception of God is not believing in His forgiveness and grace. Some people may have more difficulty with this point than others. However, this is a struggle for many people. The refusal to forgive those who have hurt us is an invitation for the enemy to walk all over us. By not entirely forgiving others, we become self-righteous or judgmental against them. We may develop anger and become irritable towards others associated or related to that person. The enemy will exploit any separation from the unconditional forgiveness by God. Many times this separation results in physical and emotional problems which are a consequence of the stronghold. I have seen countless times where people have been physically ill or physically challenged and after fully surrendering to God and releasing the unforgiveness, they are completely restored.

FALSE PERCEPTION OF YOURSELF

The second stronghold is coming into agreement with the enemy about themselves. When a person has this stronghold, they feel unworthy, dirty, guilty and often suffer from low self-esteem.

Have you ever heard someone who is always looking down at himself or herself and speaking "death" over themselves? How can a person, who was hand-made by the Creator Himself in His image, uniquely and wonderfully made, look down upon himself or herself?

Strongholds play a tremendous part in a person's struggle toward feelings of low self-esteem. Thoughts drastically affect our emotions. If you continually see yourself as a failure, you will feel like one!

Many people I've led through counseling sessions have felt worthless and condemned by their past sins even though they have been washed clean by the power of the cross. They also carry guilt and shame. Shame based thinking is another sign of this stronghold. Guilt is where somebody looks at his or her failure, but shame is where a person looks at himself or herself as the failure. A guilty conscience is found when a person doesn't perceive himself as a new creation in Christ whose sins have been washed away. If a person has a guilty conscience, he or she will feel unworthy, and this kind of thinking will kill faith.

Satan erects strongholds by exploiting situations in which we are most vulnerable. The enemy will commonly use negative childhood or traumatic experiences to create a stronghold. As children, we are more impressionable, and negative experiences leave scars, making us vulnerable in certain areas.

There are many influences that have made an impact on our lives as we grew up. These influences include parents, relatives, or other authority figures such as schoolteachers or church leaders. Other cruel children can have an influence on a young person.

These influences and experiences can lead to a weakness in our personality that the enemy can utilize to create a stronghold. You may have had an overly dominant parent. This could result in never feeling we can achieve or come up to a standard, making us perfectionists. There may have been sexual abuse that causes us to struggle with our sexuality and lack confidence in forming healthy relationships. An absent parent could lead to insecurity in developing normal relationships, especially with authority figures.

The enemy often exploits these weaknesses in us. A stronghold is erected. We then tend to think the stronghold is unchangeable and never consider that it may be brought down. We live with it not realizing the impact it has on our marriage, our family, our church, and ourselves.

A simple typical scenario is where a person feels dirty, guilty and shameful about their past. They are used to thinking about their past and are driven to think and feel like a failure. They feel undeserving of having a close intimate relationship with God. Their spiritual strength, faith, and relationship with Him are affected. No wonder the enemy tries to build such strongholds in our minds!

The enemy starts off and reminds us of our past failures and sins. He summons up things that we should not be dwelling on and tries to make us agree on how badly we failed. We have a choice to listen and agree with him, or listen to God's Word telling us that all those sins have been washed away.

If we take the bait and begin to mediate on our failures, it will begin to pull us down spiritually, and deeper strongholds will develop. We will see ourselves as failures because we've taken the bait and chosen to meditate on a lie. If you think you are a failure, you will feel like a failure. When you think you are hopeless, you will feel hopeless.

You are forgiven. When you continually think of your past failures, you will see yourself as associated with them. Think of how your past is separated from you because the Blood of Jesus washed it away.

DEMOLISHING STRONGHOLDS

Strongholds are built upon deception and lies that we've accepted into our minds. So how do you counter a lie? How do you counter deception?

With the Truth. Where do we find the Truth? In the Word of God.

In 2 Corinthians 10:3-5, we are told that our spiritual weaponry is designed to tear down strongholds:

> *"For though we live in the world, we do not wage war as the world does. The weapons we fight with are not the weapons of the world. On the contrary, they have divine power to demolish strongholds. We demolish arguments and every pretension that sets itself up against the knowledge of God, and we take captive every thought to make it obedient to Christ."*
> 2 Corinthians 10:3-5 (NIV)

When the enemy tries to condemn us and tells us, "You messed up, haven't you?" we need to stand firmly on 1 John 3:5 which states the reason Jesus went to the cross was to take away that sin. We also need to counter with Hebrews 8:12 which tells us that God has chosen to forget my sin!

Counter the lie with the Truth from God's Word. This means we need to be reading our Bible. We need to read our Bible so we can learn the Truth. We need to read our Bible, so we know the Truth.

Let's look at how Jesus rebuked the lies of the enemy.

> *Satan said to Jesus, "If thou be the Son of God, command that these stones be made bread."* Matthew 4:3 (KJV)

> *But Jesus replied with, "It is written, Man shall not live by bread alone, but by every word that proceedeth out of the mouth of God."* Matthew 4:4 (KJV)

What did Satan do? After Jesus had responded with the Truth, i.e., the Word of God, a few times, Satan had no choice but to leave defeated. His efforts were futile against Jesus! Jesus knew the appropriate scriptures to quote, and took away Satan's ability to influence Him!

Second Corinthians 10:5 (KJV) says we are to be *"cast(ing) down imaginations, and every high thing that exalteth itself against the knowledge of God, and bringing into captivity every thought to the obedience of Christ."*

The enemy plants thoughts or imaginations in our minds when he asks us a question that starts with "What if…" Don't waste your time trying to reason things out with the enemy. Just throw the thought or imagination away and get your mind on God's Word and off of what the enemy is trying to tell you.

We are to cast down every thought that comes into our minds that oppose the knowledge of God. God associates Himself with His Word (John 1:1). If anything the enemy tries to convince us of is contrary to God's Word, get rid of it! Do not waste time thinking about or trying to reason with it. If Satan is trying to tell you that God doesn't want to forgive you, then don't listen to it. Why? Because His Word says otherwise:

"Therefore the LORD longs to be gracious to you, And therefore He waits on high to have compassion on you." Isaiah 30:18 (NASB)

God wants to forgive your sins so that your relationship with Him can be restored. He genuinely desires restoration. The last thing the enemy wants us to know is God's forgiving and loving nature towards us even after we have messed up.

Stop thinking about what the enemy has been serving you, and meditate on God's Word. Take verses in the Bible that run contrary to what the enemy is saying, and repeat them to yourself out loud. The enemy built his stronghold by causing you to focus on his lies and deception. If you want to tear down a stronghold, you need to begin meditating on the exact opposite, which is God's Word.

Listening to and reasoning with the things of the enemy puts wrong thoughts in your mind. When you allow your mind to consider Satan's word it feeds strongholds. Cut him off and say NO to the garbage he's feeding you, and at the same time turn to God's Word. Begin to feed, meditate upon, think about and dwell upon on the Truth. It will stop Satan dead in his tracks!

If we do not combat these strongholds, we give a foothold to the enemy.

OPPRESSION, NOT POSSESSION

From a demonic standpoint, a stronghold can be defined as a persistent oppression, influence or grip, obsession, hindrance, or harassment.

Christians cannot be possessed by demons as we are possessed the Holy Spirit. However, Satan's army can exert influence over our lives, thoughts, and actions. When you help people walk through victory, you quite often see very sincere believers manifest demons. Not only did I witness this, but I also faced terrible demonic oppression as a believer and have been completely freed.

Demons often work in concert with strongholds to carry out their ruthless work in a person's life. There are many cases where both strongholds need to be torn down, and demons need to be cast out before the person experiences complete and lasting spiritual freedom. Demons often hide and work behind strongholds, and work at establishing and maintaining, thus making it more difficult to tear down. If a demon is a cause of a stronghold, and you are successful at tearing down the stronghold, but leave the demon, you'll likely find that stronghold keeps returning. That's because the root of the problem, the demon, wasn't addressed.

If you only cast out demons but fail to renew your mind, you will be continually harassed by those strongholds. It may not be as bad as before, but nevertheless, they can remain and torment your mind. Thus, it is important to address both demonic factors and tear down the strongholds. Anything less will often bring temporary relief and partial victory.

If a situation seems hopeless, the enemy has produced just the mindset he intended. He does this specifically by intimidating us, tempting us, exploiting our vulnerabilities and confronting us with intellectual arguments that go against gospel truths. We need to recognize that God does not intimidate, tempt, exploit or argue against Himself. When we meet the hopeless feelings that such situations provoke, Satan is at work. Learn to recognize such strongholds. Know their architect and builder is the devil.

Agree with God

We need to come into full agreement with the Bible when it comes to spiritual warfare. While it may seem like we are up against a formidable foe, remember our victory in Christ. Over the past couple of chapters, we have learned more than we have ever known about our enemy, the battlefield, his tactics, and his ability to create a division between God and us by questioning our identity in Christ.

For us to comprehend our position on the victorious battlefield with Christ, it is important to understand how God views us. Let's correct some of the lies that the enemy told us. Let's stand on His Word and His Truth. From there, we can grow stronger and live in victory.

CHAPTER SIX - RESTORING THE FOUNDATION

The world's tallest building, the Burj Khalifa opened in Dubai January 4, 2010. At a staggering 2,717 feet tall – more than half a mile high - it easily overshadows the previous tallest building Taipei in Taiwan at 1,671 feet tall and stands double the height of the renowned Empire State Building.

Accommodating 12,000 people, the Burj Khalifa, built at a cost of $1.5 billion, captured several other world records. While most attention focuses on its height, perhaps more important is what lies buried beneath the building. Without a solid foundation, the world's tallest building would become the world's longest pile of rubble. Extending 164 feet deep under the Burj Khalifa is 58,900 cubic yards of concrete weighing over 120,000 tons. It took a year just to build the foundation.

So it is with great lives. What people see - what we marvel about – are the great heights to which some people seem to soar. Yet, supporting any truly great life is a solid foundation. A heralded career is built on foundational principles like dependability and hard work. A celebrated sixtieth wedding anniversary results from deep love and selflessness. Successful retirement depends on years of responsible money management.

Jesus said, *"Everyone who hears these words of mine and puts them into practice is like a wise man who built his house on the rock. The rain came down, the streams rose, and the winds blew and beat against that house; yet it did not fall, because it had its foundation on the rock"* Matthew 7:24-25 (ESV)

Foundation matters. We cannot start wrong and expect to finish right. Remember to start with a solid foundation[1].

At this point, you may have come to the revelation that you inadvertently come into agreement with the enemy.

> *"And you will know the truth, and the truth will set you free."* John 8:32 (ESV)

The key to living of a life of victory in Christ is having a clear understanding of our position with Christ and the love He has for us. Have a clear understanding of who we are IN CHRIST.

The opposite of truth are false beliefs that the enemy used to deceive you. These lies will cause you to live unnecessarily in bondage. If you see yourself as a failure, you will feel unworthy, and thus may not be able to exercise your authority in Christ boldly.

I want you to say to yourself, "I am worthy, because JESUS' death on the cross has made me worthy!"

Love by God the Father

God loves you because of who you are, not because of what you've done. He desired a relationship with us even before we came into this world.

> *"But God shows his love for us in that while we were still sinners, Christ died for us"* Romans 5:8 (ESV)

It may be hard to get your mind around, but it is true. God loves us with the same love that He had towards Jesus Himself.

> *"I in them and you in me, that they may become perfectly one, so that the world may know that you sent me and loved them even as you loved me."* John 17:23 (ESV)

Jesus said that the greatest love a man can show for his friends is when he lays down his life for them. Because of how valuable and dear we are to Him, Jesus laid down His life for us.

> *"Greater love has no one than this, that someone lay down his life for his friends."* John 15:13 (ESV)

To grasp the fullness of God, we need to realize God's love fully. We will lack the fullness of His presence in our lives until we come to know of His deep love for us.

> *"So that Christ may dwell in your hearts through faith—that you, being rooted and grounded in love, may have strength to comprehend with all the saints what is the breadth and length and height and depth, and to know the love of Christ that surpasses knowledge, that you may be filled with all the fullness of God."* Ephesians 3:17-19 (ESV)

The wages of your sin was death (Romans 6:23), but Jesus paid that price for you. God's Word tells us that we were purchased by the precious Blood of the Lamb:

> *"For you were bought with a price. So glorify God in your body."* 1 Corinthians 6:20 (ESV)

> *"And they sang a new song, saying, Worthy are you to take the scroll and to open its seals, for you were slain, and by your blood you ransomed people for God from every tribe and language and people and nation."* Revelations 5:9 (ESV)

Jesus purchased us with His blood because of His deep love for us, and His desire to have a relationship with you and I based on that love.

> *"But God shows his love for us in that while we were still sinners, Christ died for us."* Romans 5:8 (ESV)

We are justified and declared innocent when we have repented of our sins and accepted the gift of God. The forgiveness of sins is accomplished through the precious shed Blood of Christ. At that point, God's Word tells you that you are justified.

> *"Yet we know that a person is not justified by works of the law but through faith in Jesus Christ, so we also have believed in Christ Jesus, in order to be justified by faith in Christ and not by works of the law, because by works of the law no one will be justified."* Galatians 2:16 (ESV)

The word "justified" in the above passage is derived from the Greek word *dikaioo*, which means, "to render (that is, show or regard as) just or innocent: - free, justify (-ier), be righteous.[2]" If a person is justified, it means they are made innocent or made just as if they have never sinned.

We are entitled to have a clean conscience. Because our sins have been removed from us, we are justified, made right with God. You and I entitled to a clean and unspoiled conscience despite what the enemy tries to get us to believe.

> *"How much more will the blood of Christ, who through the eternal Spirit offered himself without blemish to God, purify our conscience from dead works to serve the living God?"* Hebrews 9:14 (ESV)

You deny the work that Christ did for you whenever you beat yourself up over your past failures which have been nailed to the cross. A clean conscience before the Lord agrees with what Christ did in removing your sin and declaring you innocent and justified before the Lord.

Your sins are no longer a part of you. Your sins have not merely been covered, but truly removed from your account. This was not possible in the Old Testament, but through the precious Blood of Christ, the removal of sins is a reality.

> *"The next day he saw Jesus coming toward him, and said, "Behold, the Lamb of God, who takes away the sin of the world!"* John 1:29 (ESV)

> *"For this is my blood of the covenant, which is poured out for many for the forgiveness of sins."* Matthew 26:28 (ESV)

Beyond forgiving, God Himself chose to forget our failures. When He sees us as His precious children, who stand blameless before Him, not our failures as we often feel He sees us.

> *"I will remember their sins and their lawless deeds no more."* Hebrews 10:17 (ESV)

Our relationship with God is restored. We are justified and made right with God. We can boldly enter His presence with a clean conscience because of our faith in Christ Jesus and the work that He did for us on the cross.

> *"Therefore, since we have been justified by faith, we have peace with God through our Lord Jesus Christ."* Romans 5:1 (ESV)

We are clothed in the righteousness of Jesus. As believers in Christ, a great exchange has taken place; our sin for Jesus' righteousness.

> *"Even the righteousness of God which is by faith of Jesus Christ unto all and upon all them that believe: for there is no difference."* Romans 3:22 (KJV)

> *"Whom God put forward as a propitiation by his blood, to be received by faith. This was to show God's righteousness, because in his divine forbearance he had passed over former sins."* Romans 3:25 (ESV)

> *"For if, because of one man's trespass, death reigned through that one man, much more will those who receive the abundance of grace and the free gift of righteousness reign in life through the one man Jesus Christ."* Romans 5:17 (ESV)

Jesus received punishment for our sins, which was what we deserved. In exchange, however, He gave us His righteousness.

You are made new in Christ, born of God. The old saying, "We are just forgiven sinners saved by grace" is so misleading because it denies the work that God has done for us. Our identity is not a "forgiven sinner". We are a new creation in Christ Jesus, old things having passed away and all things have become new.

> *"Therefore, if anyone is in Christ, he is a new creation. The old has passed away; behold, the new has come."* 2 Corinthians 5:17 (ESV)

When you accept Jesus as your Lord and Savior and believe in Him, you become a new creation in Christ. God's Word tells us that this new creation is founded in righteousness and true holiness:

> *"And to put on the new self, created after the likeness of God in true righteousness and holiness."* Ephesians 4:24 (ESV)

When we are born again, we have become sons and daughters of God.

> *"But to all who did receive him, who believed in his name, he gave the right to become children of God, who were born, not of blood nor of the will of the flesh nor of the will of man, but of God."* John 1:12-13 (ESV)

So what happened to the "old" you? The "old" you was crucified with Christ. God didn't repair the "old" you. He created a "new" you in Christ. This is what the Bible means when it talks about being born again.

> *"Jesus answered, "Truly, truly, I say to you, unless one is born of water and the Spirit, he cannot enter the kingdom of God. That which is born of the flesh is flesh, and that which is born of the Spirit is spirit. Do not marvel that I said to you, 'You must be born again.'."* John 3:5-7 (ESV)

> *"I have been crucified with Christ. It is no longer I who live, but Christ who lives in me. And the life I now live in the flesh I live by faith in the Son of God, who loved me and gave himself for me."* Galatians 2:20 (ESV)

Many people do not realize that we are seated with Christ who sits in a position of authority. Jesus is seated at the right hand of God. God's Word tells us that we are seated with Christ. Therefore, we are seated in the same position of authority.

> *"And raised us up with him and seated us with him in the heavenly places in Christ Jesus."* Ephesians 2:6 (ESV)

Because of this position with and in Christ, we have authority over all sickness, diseases, and demons. Luke 10:17-20 states that according to Jesus *"that signs and wonders would follow those who believe, including casting out demons."* Look at what the Gospel of Mark states:

> *"And he said to them, "Go into all the world and proclaim the gospel to the whole creation. Whoever believes and is baptized will be saved, but whoever does not believe will be condemned. And these signs will accompany those who believe: in my name they will cast out demons; they will speak in new tongues; they will pick up serpents with their hands; and if they drink any deadly poison, it will not hurt them; they will lay their hands on the sick, and they will recover."* Mark 16:15-18 (ESV)

Who shall these signs follow? Them that BELIEVE. That means all true followers of Christ that are alive on the earth right now.

> *"And they sang a new song, saying, 'Worthy are you to take the scroll and to open its seals, for you were slain, and by your blood you ransomed people for God from every tribe and language and people and nation, and you have made them a kingdom and priests to our God, and they shall reign on the earth.'"* Revelation 5:9-10 (ESV)

Because we have God-given authority, we can speak with authority over sickness and command it to flee in Jesus' name. We can command broken bones to grow. We don't need to "ask" God to heal somebody. We can speak in faith, confidence, and with authority in Jesus name.

The New Testament tells how Jesus, His disciples, and the early church exercised their faith when they went out to heal the sick. They didn't ask the Father to heal the sick. They said things like, *"Be healed in Jesus' name"* or *"Rise and walk!"*

It was standard practice for the early followers of Christ to go out and heal the sick and to cast out demons. That hasn't changed in today's environment, although the enemy has led many to believe it has. We must take the authority that Christ has given us, and exercise it through faith in Jesus' name.

Jesus made it clear that we have authority here on earth through our position of being seated with Him. Jesus illustrated this when he cursed the fig tree:

> *"Now in the morning as he returned into the city, he hungered. And when he saw a fig tree in the way, he came to it, and found nothing thereon, but leaves only, and said unto it, Let no fruit grow on thee henceforward forever. And presently the fig tree withered away. And when the disciples saw it, they marveled, saying, How soon is the fig tree withered away! Jesus answered and said unto them, Verily I say unto you, If ye have faith, and doubt not, ye shall not only do this which is done to the fig tree, but also if ye shall say unto this mountain, Be thou removed, and be thou cast into the sea; it shall be done. And all things, whatsoever ye shall ask in prayer, believing, ye shall receive."* Matthew 21:18-22 (KJV)

When you don't realize who you are in Christ, your faith will be hindered. If you don't feel worthy to exercise your authority in Christ, then you won't act in the fullness of faith. The enemy works diligently to fool people's minds to feel unworthy and unable to walk in the power of God here on earth.

The feeling of unworthiness is one of the most powerful and prevalent strongholds in existence today in the body of Christ. By our own power and effort, we are unworthy. But the Blood of Christ that makes us worthy.

It is when we obey the Lord and trust in God do we emerge victorious against our enemy. We face battles in our lives today. Not on a field with swords and spears, but in our hearts and minds.

We will only be victorious when we are obedient to what God has revealed to us. If you do not see victories in your life, you may be ignoring the fact that you are not obedient to God's Word. Maybe you are trusting in the Lord today, but suffer the consequences of past disobedience and strongholds.

Let's look at some examples in the Old Testament where battles took place in the physical realm and see what we can learn from them about the spiritual.

PART TWO
THE BATTLES

CHAPTER SEVEN - LEARNING FROM THE PAST

You may have heard the phrase, "those who do not learn from the past are doomed to repeat it." We do have an uncanny way of making the same mistakes over and over again, and wondering why we don't learn something about it.

When we look at the Old Testament, we see a nation chosen by God experience numerous cycles of rebellion and reconciliation. I know in my life, I can point to many times where I have allowed the enemy to create separation from God through rebellion.

I was recently drawn to Acts 7:1-53 where Stephen, filled and moved by the Holy Spirit addressed the Sanhedrin. The Sanhedrin was the supreme council and tribunal of the Jews during post-exilic times headed by a High Priest with religious, civil, and criminal jurisdiction.

Stephen starts describing a historical account of Israel. He speaks of Abraham as the father of the nation of Israel. He explains how the

Israelites came to Egypt through Joseph's story. Stephen then shares the story of Moses. He then ends with a brief mention of Joshua and David and Solomon.

Then, Stephen presents his conclusion summary of why he shared Israel's history: *"You stiff-necked people, uncircumcised in heart and ears, you always resist the Holy Spirit. As your fathers did, so do you. Which of the prophets did not your fathers persecute? And they killed those who announced beforehand the coming of the Righteous One [Jesus], whom you have now betrayed and murdered, you who received the law as delivered by angels and did not keep it"* (Acts 7:51–53)

Stephen states that Israel *"always resists the Holy Spirit."* God had been restoring Israel with repeated acts of mercy and patience. Israel had hardened their hearts, *"stiffened their necks"*, and stopped listening to God. In one word of the Scripture, we can summarize this story of Israel's relationship with God; it is rebellious.

God wants us to be encouraged by seeing His patience with the rebellious nation of Israel. God is *"slow to anger and abounding in steadfast love and forgives iniquity and transgression and sin"* (Exodus 34:6–7). God is not eager to punish but longs to forgive and encourages us to become repentant and humble.

But there is a warning that we need to heed from Stephen's narrative. These are the words of verse 42 of Acts 7: *"God turned and gave them over to worship the host of heaven."* If we resist the Holy Spirit's work in our life to convict us of sin, there will be an end to God's patience. He will hand us over to the power of our sin if we keep rejecting his mercy and grace.

God wants to awaken us to this fearsome truth: If we resist Him for too long and desire other things more than we desire Him, then He may do what he did with the nation of Israel. He left them to their own sin: turned away, stop convicting, stop giving the feelings of guilt. This gives a foothold to the enemy. We get what we have been asking for.

God's patience, as well as the warnings of judgment, are both works of grace. We need to make sure we perceive it as such.

God is not going to force Himself on us. He desires so much for us to have a personal and deep relationship with Him. He is full of grace and mercy, but because of that, we have to make the choice to turn from sin and to follow Him.

The best way to heed God's encouragement and warning is to learn from Israel's history where we see both their rebellion and His mercy. I encourage you to get out your Bible and follow along as we dive into the history of Israel and see the parallels in our own lives.

Abraham

In looking at the history of Israel more objectively, let's begin at about the middle of verse 2 in Acts 7 on the call of Abraham. *"The God of glory appeared to our father Abraham, when he was in Mesopotamia before he lived in Haran, and said to him, 'Depart from your land and from your kindred and go into the land which I will show you.'"* Abraham obeys the Lord but makes his journey half way into the Promised Land and settled in Haran (Acts 4:2-4).

But God being patient with Abraham helps him along to get to the Promised land. In Verse 4b it states *"And after his father died, God removed him from there into this land in which you are now living."*

God's mercy begins with selecting Abraham out of all the people on the earth to inherit the Promised Land. God's patience starts with giving Abraham an extra push to get all the way to the Promised Land when he had settled halfway in Haran.

Joseph

Continuing on, the next story of importance was the move of Joseph, one of Abraham's great-grandsons, to Egypt. *"And the patriarchs, jealous of Joseph, sold him into Egypt."* (v. 9) Joseph's brothers were jealous and insecure about the way God was speaking Joseph. He dreams implied that someday, they would have to bow down to him. God was showing them the future to prepare them for the famine, but they were not able to see that. They were hardened in their hearts and were resistance to God's will for their life.

For all they did to Joseph, the Scripture says: *"But God was with him, and rescued him out of all his afflictions, and gave him favor and wisdom before Pharaoh, king of Egypt, who made him governor over Egypt"* (verses 9b–10).

Invariably, in and through the jealousy and resistance of Joseph's brothers, God was still patient and merciful. Despite the fact that they rejected God's word in Joseph's dreams, God, instead of judging them, used their sin to rescue to them when they ran out of food and had to come begging in Egypt and to their brother.

Moses

In the wisdom of God, when Joseph had played his part in bringing about the outworking of the purpose of God for the Hebrew people, God raised up another person by the name Moses as a deliverer for His oppressed people in Egypt. But when Moses attempted to help the Israelites, they resisted him. This is clearly brought out when Moses tried to solve a conflict between two Israelites: *"Men, you are brethren, why do you wrong each other?" But the man who was wronging his neighbor thrust him aside, saying, 'Who made you a ruler and a judge over us?'"* (verses 26-27)

Stephen points out that the nation of Israel rejected Moses as their deliverer and correlates that with the religious people of his time rejected of Jesus, who was God's gift of mercy and grace.

Back to the story, Moses fled into exile to the land of Midian. Again, God's patience and mercy met Moses sent him back to the same people who rejected him in the first place. *"I have surely seen the ill-treatment of my people that are in Egypt and heard their groaning, and I have come down to deliver them. And now come, I will send you to Egypt"* (v. 34).

In Stephen's story at verse 36, we see Moses leading the nation of Israel out of the bondage of Egypt: *"He led them out, having performed wonders and signs in Egypt and at the Red Sea, and in the wilderness for forty years."*

ISRAEL'S WILDERNESS EXPERIENCE

God repeatedly showed patience and mercy to the nation of Israel. *"Our fathers refused to obey him [Moses], but thrust him aside, and in their hearts they turned to Egypt, saying to Aaron, 'Make for us gods to go before us; as for this Moses who led us out from the land of Egypt, we do not know what has become of him.' And they made a calf in those days, and offered a sacrifice to the idol and rejoiced in the works of their hands"* (verses 39–41).

Regrettably and unfortunately for many of the Israelites, God's patience came to an end at that point. *"God turned and gave them over to worship the host of heaven"* (v. 42).

They rejected worshipping and relying on God and wanted idols made with their hands. God gave them up to the reality behind all idols, which are demonic spirits. Verse 34 states, *"You took up the tent of Moloch, and the star of the god Rephan."* These were false gods and demonic spirits prevalent in that region.

Even after all that, God did not stop showing mercy to the Israelites. The Scripture says that Israel *"dispossessed the nations which God thrust out before our fathers"* as they entered into the Promised Land. Even after their failure in the wilderness, God fought for the nation of Israel by helping to drive out the existing nations in the Promised Land. Even then, the nation of Israel did not obey God's commands completely to remove all evil in the land, which comes back to cause numerous problems in Israel's history.

What an amazing God we have. Even in the midst of all of our junk, of willingly turning away from God, He is faithful and just to redeem us.

Made by Hands

After bringing his audience through the history of Israel, Stephen gets to the point of the accusation against him. He states that Solomon built God a house, a temple they highly valued and that Jesus said he would destroy and build again in three days. And Stephen wrapped it up when he said that in all this: *"Yet the Most High does not dwell in houses made with hands"* (v. 48).

Stephen was linking the sin of Israel, their resistance to God's will, to the fact they derived their joy, fulfillment, meaning, purpose, and sense of significance from what they could achieve by themselves. It states in verse 41 that they *"rejoiced in the works of their hands."*

This was the root cause of their resistance to God's will. This is why they resisted the Holy Spirit as he claims in verse 51.

They wanted independence from God so they could exhibit their own power, wisdom, righteousness, morality and their religious zeal. They obtained joy from what they could achieve on their own apart from God.

Thus, the temple in Jerusalem at that time became a symbol of what the religious zealots could achieve—the work of their hands. The worship there had become a form of self-worship. While all were very religious, saying the right words, it came from impure hearts and stiff, unsubmissive and self-exalting thoughts. Sound like any church you know?

Jesus Destroyed the Temple

Jesus said He would destroy the temple and build another in three days *"not made with hands,"* Mark 14:58. He was referring to how he would destroy the kind of religion that focuses on works and efforts.

Stephen did not boast about his achievements of his own hands or the performances of his own power. Instead, he focused on God in faith and relied on the Holy Spirit for power, so that God would get all the glory.

Lessons Learned

We can learn a lot from the history surrounding God's dealings with the children of Israel. It serves as an example to us today that God is consistent in His nature and does not change. The Scriptures say that God is, *"slow to anger and abounding in steadfast love, showing faithfulness to thousands and forgiving iniquity and transgression and sin."* He does not turn from us or stop pursuing us because we have sinned once, twice, ten times or seventy times or seventy times seven times. You can still repent, and He is still pursuing you. That is amazing!

Now don't misunderstand. It is not like we are taking God for granted. We are drawing conclusions after careful examination of His character as seen in the Scripture. We have no other way of knowing God except by what the Word says about Him. The Scripture says that God's anger is but for a moment but that His mercy endures forever (Psalm 30:5; Psalm 136). This shows us the nature of God. He can be angry as long as we stay in our sin. But when we repent and get back to Him, He forgets and then returns by default to His merciful and loving kindness nature.

God's mercy out weighs His anger. We can count on that as long as we are repentant and in tune with His ways and heart. He wants our hearts more than He does our actions. This should cause us to make a greater effort to stay in righteousness. We will not lose our salvation when we sin. However, instead of repeating the same mistakes over and over again, and returning to our sins, let's learn from the past, and look at how God's Word provides a pathway to ultimate freedom in Christ.

As we dive deeper into specific areas of Israel's past, I want you to pay close attention to how God reacts. Yes, out of righteous anger and disappointment, but ALWAYS with a path towards repentance, no matter what. We can learn from our past. You will see some strategies to put into practice as we analyze four specific Old Testament battles.

CHAPTER EIGHT - GIDEON

I remember in my young teenage years when I was over at a friend's house. Just like many teenage boys, he had found his parents' Playboy magazine and decided to show it off to us. It was a quick look, but it was an open door that took ahold of my life.

That first look grabbed a portion of my soul in such a way that even when I closed my eyes, I would continually see the pictures. In no time, a stronghold was formed, and a battle was fought. Pornography became an addiction that I couldn't find release from.

Over time, it grew into a massive stronghold. The things that I saw messed me up on the inside. My curiosity grew and over time led to a point where I almost lost my marriage.

But I never wanted and liked what I was doing. And you can be sure that if you are born again, the Holy Spirit will quickly convict you of sin and prompt you to repent. I did that with tears and wished I had never seen pornography. I would come to God most times in tears and repentance asking God to help me. Sometimes I would have victory over it for a few months, but then I would be back to it again and again. This went on for over thirty years. I can tell you the many ways it crippled my spirit and, of course, the many other branches that grew on that stump.

What started as a simple look at pornography in my friend's room become a mountain and a battle of falling and rising and falling and rising resulting in shame and loss of confidence in the presence of God and His people. But mercy came to my rescue when I became desperate and utterly helpless.

WILLFUL SIN

We willfully sin. We are disobedient to God. We do not have a mean and angry God, but we do have a just GOD.

Maybe you are struggling with habitual sin. Maybe you are like I was struggling to break free from pornography, masturbation, fornication, lying, and stealing even as a born again believer.

Maybe you struggle with anger, doubt, fear or things in your life you know that are not from God. These are things you've probably now identified as strongholds based on Part One of this book.

Maybe, like me, you have fasted and asked God to kill the parts of your body that are causing you sin. Maybe you have even gone to your pastor to confess and own up to him so that you wouldn't be hiding it anymore and yet nothing is breaking.

And maybe after a lot of repenting and repenting, you have finally resolved that it is not working and that you are fooling yourself but do not want to keep fooling God. So you feel like you should pack your bags and lay down to sleep in that mud of sin like a pig and a dog that has returned to its vomit. You feel like there is no hope, no way out of this endless cycle.

The good news is that there is a way out for you. Maybe now you've begun to realize that even at this point. Hold on to that promise! I want to show you that you are not alone. All hope is NOT lost. Let's look at a man named Gideon. He was the sixth judge discussed in the book of Judges. If you are like me, reading the book of Judges quickly put you to sleep. However, there are so many rich lessons from Gideon's story that can help us achieve victory. Look for yourself in his story then look to God for his redemptive grace and mercy.

The story of Gideon is recorded in Judges 6:1-8:35. A detailed description of the Midianites' oppression of the Israelites precedes the story of Gideon. Here we find Gideon called to become a judge to the nation of Israel.

Gideon's Call

Gideon was called while threshing wheat near his father's terebinth tree in Ophrah. The Scripture says that the Angel of the Lord appeared to him and gave a beautiful but surprising message and truth: that the Lord was with him. Gideon questioned the reality of God's presence with Israel who, under the dominion of the Midianites, had not seen the Lord work any great miracles.

When God exhorted Gideon to go and save Israel from the Midianites, Gideon immediately informed the Lord of his inadequacies and requested that the Lord give him a sign. Gideon, who knew so well about blood sacrifices, prepared his offering to offer to the Lord. He was aware that if it were indeed the Lord directing him, He would accept his offering. Then Gideon prepared an offering as a way of testing the veracity of the words and his visitor. When the Angel of the Lord touched the offering with the end of his staff, fire came out of the rock and consumed the offering and immediately, the Angel disappeared.

Gideon despaired of seeing the Angel of the Lord face-to-face because he knew from Scripture that no man ever saw the face of the Lord and lived. But God, loving as He always is, quickly assured him that he would not die. Then Gideon, in response, built an altar to the Lord, who spared his life and named it "The Lord is Peace."

Gideon's Destruction of the Baal Altar

The first instruction the Lord gave to Gideon was to destroy his father's Baal altar and Asherah image and then to build another altar to the Lord. He was instructed to use the wood of the Asherah image to offer a burnt offering on the altar. Because Gideon was afraid of his father's house and the men of the city, Gideon and ten of his servants carried out these instructions during the night.

When the men of the city awoke the next morning and discovered the destroyed altar, they demanded that Joash the Abiezrite, Gideon's father, hand over his son so that they could execute him. Joash denied their request and told them that if Baal was a god, he could defend himself. Joash then changed Gideon's name to Jerubbaal, which means "Let Baal Contend."

Gideon's Battle with the Midianites

It is interesting how Gideon battled with the enemies of Israel. The Scripture says that when the Midianites and Amalekites invaded and encamped in the Valley of Jezreel, Gideon, empowered by the Spirit of the Lord, sounded his trumpet and sent messengers to Manasseh, Asher, Zebulun, and Naphtali and then the Abiezrites and the other four tribes gathered with him.

At this point, as has almost become the custom of Gideon, he requested a sign that the Lord would use him to deliver Israel. Gideon told the Lord that if he put a fleece on the threshing room floor and if there was dew on the fleece but the ground was dry then that would be the sign. God granted this. Not entirely satisfied, Gideon again desiring one more sign, asked the Lord to do the opposite the next night; the next morning the fleece was dry, and the ground was covered in dew.

Gideon and his army encamped against the Midianites at the well of Harod. But God reduced Gideon's army to three hundred men to prevent Israel from claiming glory for itself. Remember this was one of the things that Stephen said about the children of Israel - they always wanted to do things on their own and by their efforts and strength so they could take pride in their ability. But God is never in support of this kind of attitude.

God commanded Gideon to go into the camp of the Midianites and Amalekites. Gideon and his servant, Purah, entered into the enemy camp, where they overheard a man discussing a dream with his companion. In the man's dream, he saw a loaf of bread tumbling into the Midianite camp and knocking down a tent. His companion immediately interpreted the dream as the Midianites being delivered into the hand of Gideon. Upon hearing this conversation, Gideon worshiped the Lord and returned to prepare his men for battle.

But Gideon had to be strategic in battle. He divided his men into three groups and gave each man a trumpet, a pitcher, and a torch. The three groups went down to the outpost of the camp, blew their trumpets, broke their pitchers, held their torches, and shouted, *"The sword of the Lord and of Gideon."* When Gideon and his men blew their trumpets, the men of the enemy camp began killing one another, and their armies fled.

As Gideon's army set out in pursuit, Gideon sent messengers to the men of Ephraim requesting their assistance. The men of Ephraim took control of the watering places in front of the Midianites, captured and killed two of their princes, and brought their heads back to Gideon. But when the men of Ephriam became upset because Gideon had not invited them when he first attacked, Gideon pointed out that their capture of the Midian princes was more important than his acts.

GIDEON'S PURSUIT OF THE KINGS OF MIDIAN

Gideon and his army continued their chase after the two kings of Midian - Zebah and Zalmunna. During their pursuit, Gideon and his men stopped at two cities to request bread.

When both cities denied their request, Gideon swore vengeance: he promised the men of Succoth that he would return and beat them with briers and thorns, and he promised the men of Penuel that he would come back and tear down their tower. After Gideon's army had defeated the two kings, Gideon fulfilled his promises to the men of Succoth and Penuel.

Gideon interrogated a man from Succoth to learn the names of Succoth's leaders. He then interrogated the kings of Midian, who admitted to killing his brothers. When Gideon's firstborn son, Jether, was afraid to kill the kings as ordered, Gideon carried out the slaughter himself and took the ornaments from their camels' necks.

GIDEON'S EPHOD

Due to Gideon's triumph and victory in battle over the Midianites, the Israelites asked Gideon to rule over them. But Gideon refused and informed them that the Lord would be their ruler. However, he requested they bring him the earrings they gained from the plunder. The men gave him 1,700 shekels of gold earrings, with which Gideon made an ephod and erected it in the city of Ophrah. Strangely, the man through whom God gained victory over the enemies of Israel lapsed into idolatry, a strong form of resistance to God. Consequently, this ephod became a stumbling block for Gideon and all of Israel.

GIDEON'S DEATH NOTICE

It is alarming how a person can be a giant with the Lord today and then fall into stupidity, foolishness and timidity tomorrow. This is not just the case of Gideon alone. Some of the great prophets, Elijah, Samuel and even Moses and David, had their ups and down. But the saving grace in their lives was that they were repentant and God in His mercy and grace still rescued them when they called out to Him.

Now the story of Gideon closes with a summary of events. Israel enjoyed rest for forty years during Gideon's time as a judge. Gideon had seventy sons, including Abimelech, the next Ruler and Judge of Israel. Gideon was buried in his father's tomb in Ophrah. After Gideon's death, Israel returned to Baal worship and treated Gideon's family with contempt.

We Are Like Gideon

Undoubtedly, the history of Gideon has a central position within the book of Judges. Gideon's story represents a turning point in the book concerning the character of the judges of Israel because the judges before Gideon are presented in a positive light and those that followed are not. Gideon is portrayed in a positive light at times and a negative light on other occasions.

Given the placement of Gideon's story in Judges, we can see how Gideon's personal struggle to believe God's promise had an effect on the nation of Israel, and the other judges as well.

Gideon and Israel

Gideon's life parallels the people to whom he is sent to deliver. What we see in Gideon's behavior in questioning God mimics the nation of Israel's spiritual journey. Although Gideon began by tearing down his father's Baal altar, he ended his judgeship by making a golden ephod, which caused the nation to stumble. As such, Israel consistently repented of false worship, yet quickly faded back into idolatry.

We too are like the Nation of Israel - oppressed and longing for deliverance, but hesitant to follow the Lord. Many of us mirror both

Israel and Gideon in the fact that we many times demonstrate great fearfulness yet refuse to abandon those things that keep us in bondage.

Human beings have not changed. We can see the culture of our day in the nation of Israel during Gideon's time. Many believers are oppressed, tormented, beaten down by sin, deadly habits, and Satan. We long for deliverance, repent, and cry out to the Lord now and then, but, rebellion and independence remain in our very hearts. We want to continue to have our way just like the children of Israel and not want to submit completely to the Lord and follow His way fully.

CHOOSE TO CHANGE

We cannot say that we have indeed learned if we do not change. We need to heed the warning from the story above. Sin results in bondage. Israel's sin left her powerless before the enemy. Sin brings you into the spiritual bondage of the enemy. The enemy cannot have a person until he has successful lured them into sin and then have the person exposes himself to his attacks.

RESTORATION COMES FROM GOD

The Midianite oppression brought Israel to the place where they finally sought God for deliverance. When the enemy has taken you captive through your sin, God is your only hope of restoration. I think most of the time God allows things to happen in our lives so we may ultimately look for Him.

I am not saying that God is pleased with the thing that He allows into your life. You and I know that God hates sin and will never condone it although you can open the door of your life to sin and the enemy. However, God loves you, and His mercy is still flowing in your direction; He will get the glory for Himself in bringing you out of it.

So the wisdom is this: if you have been taken captive by sin and Satan, stop running and struggling by yourself to be free. Come to God in humble submission, and He will rescue and restore you; he is your only hope now.

GET ALONE WITH GOD

Some of the great men of Scripture knew the secret of getting alone with God and became great that way. Jacob was one of them. In the story of Gideon, we see that Gideon was by himself when he was commissioned to deliver Israel.

Valiant leaders of spiritual warfare must spend time alone with God. If you are to help others through this type ministry, this strategy is vital because when you are alone God communicates His secrets to you. Husbands talk to their wives differently in their bedroom than they do in public. God is the same way.

PULL DOWN THE ALTARS OF IDOLATRY

Gideon pulled down and destroyed the altars of Baal. You are to pull down the strongholds of the enemy and destroy every idolatrous thing that stands in the way of total commitment to God. I advise you not to take this point lightly. There are so many idols in our lives and hearts today that need to be pulled down.

Yours might not necessarily be a physical image, but what about that idol of money that is standing between you and God? What about the idol of that man or that woman that is not the will of God for you to marry or date, yet you stick to him or her in complete defiance to the nudging of the Holy Spirit?

We have got to destroy all these idols and let God have His way in our life. What in your life has become your idol? Recognize also that there may be some actual physical idols in your house, a statue, that have a higher place than your Lord. Remove those!

Be endured by the Spirit of God

If you look critically at the judges, you will discover one thread that connects them together, a common denominator in all their lives. It is the Spirit of God. All the judges and, of course, Gideon were empowered by the Holy Spirit to accomplish the divine purpose and tasks assigned by God.

Our story must be different than the Nation of Israel if we are going to win the battles over our lives. Thus, the endowment of power by the Holy Spirit must come upon you for the same reason.

Seek deeper levels of faith

God is willing to put up with our growth and excesses in the pursuit of His purpose. Because we are not all at the same level of faith at the same time when God calls us, some of us may want to see visible signs of the presence of the Lord before they take Him at His Word and step out in obedience to His Word. He will do for you what will help your faith and belief, but ultimately, He wants you to trust and take Him at His Word as a child.

Feelings and signs can and will change, but the Word of God abides forever and thus it is the only authentic instruction. Gideon needed a fleece as a sign to be willing to trust God. Some Christians cannot believe unless they have certain affirmative signs in the natural world. Nonetheless, you need to seek a deeper level of faith that takes God at His Word even when natural circumstances are contrary. It is okay to ask for signs, but also it is important to move forward in faith. One of my favorite sayings is that "God doesn't move a parked car." We have to take the first step of faith, and I am confident God will reward you with a sign.

Do not be self-reliant

I love the way God works. He will always want to work in a way that only Him, and no one else can share and get glory in the things that He does. He knows that man is always tempted and quick to believe in his ability and strength of power and would end up exalting himself as god because he is able to get some things done.

We see God preventing this act of self-reliance by reducing the army of Gideon to a small number, from 3,000 able-bodied men to only 300 men That is humorous!

But that is God for you. He will work in your life to eliminate self-reliance so you will recognize that the victory and all victories come from Him.

Do not hesitate

Humans being have not changed and may never change. How many times has God told you to do some things and instead of stepping out in the obedience and faith, you still hesitated for three months, maybe two, and sometimes ten years? Man has not changed.

In spite of God's confirmations, we notice that Gideon still hesitated to face the enemy. Of course, he had never led an army before, and his men were untrained and inexperienced but was that enough to stay home after God told him to step out?

There are times when you may hesitate to move in a new direction God has told you to go. You may feel inexperienced and inadequate. Do not hesitate any further. You are not alone in this venture. And one thing is certain - God equips those He calls.

Target the fear of the enemy

In strategic warfare, one must know the weakness of his enemy and then take advantage of it if he is to win the battle over the enemy. Do not forget this: the thing you fear is also afraid of you and everybody and every army formation have a loophole, a weakness that if exploited will give one the upper hand over the adversary. Thus, God, the greatest military strategist, allowed Gideon to hear the fears of the Midianites. That is why James 2:19 says that the devil believe in God and tremble in fear. Therefore, we are to target the fear of the enemy with the power of God, and if we do so, we will bring the enemy down.

The God of Israel and the God of Today

I see God running down the foes with His fierce army in battle. I see the blood of the slain enemy of God spilled and running on the streets. God is up to it again. He is calling us to repent and come back to Him for His strength and wisdom to face the battles of life.

What we see in the life and story of Gideon is nothing compared to what God will do with the body of Christ if we individually and collectively turn from willful sin into the place of obedience and faith in God, following hard after Him.

God has not changed a bit. He is the Lord that does not change. We see that every time Israel repented and turned their backs on idolatry and willful sin to God, He always came through for them with victories and triumph on every side. The church is likened to the children of Israel in the wilderness and their life's journey. We have a lot to learn from the Israelites and what God did for them when they turned to Him from sin; they were victorious and triumphant over their enemies. God will do this for us today too.

A passage in the book of Isaiah will help to communicate what I see in my spirit if the church would wholeheartedly turn to God again from willful sins of pride and self-sufficiency.

> *'Who is this who comes from Edom, in crimsoned garments from Bozrah, he who is splendid in his apparel, marching in the greatness of his strength？ 'It is I, speaking in righteousness, mighty to save.' Why is your apparel red, and your garments like his who treads in the winepress？ 'I have trodden the winepress alone, and from the peoples no one was with me;*

I trod them in my anger and trampled them in my wrath; their lifeblood spattered on my garments, and stained all my apparel. For the day of vengeance was in my heart, and my year of redemption had come.'" Isaiah 63:1-4 (ESV)

Wouldn't that bring about a complete and radical change in our lives, families and communities? I think so!

CHAPTER NINE - AHAZ & HEZEKIAH

If we were to look at your life as your house, how would you describe it? I imagine that it would look like mine did - great and good-looking on the outside. And if I decided to let you in, I'm only going to let you into my front living room where everything is perfectly arranged. However, I'd never let you look into my bedroom, and especially not the closet.

Sometimes our rooms are a mess.

You know what else gets cluttered up, and messy like our rooms sometimes are? Our hearts and our minds! Sin clutters our spiritual rooms; stuff from our past adds to the disarray. We need to clean up our hearts and minds — our "rooms" — more often than we have been doing.

But the question is: how should we go about this cleaning?

In three different books of the Old Testament, we find two kings; a father, Ahaz, and his son, Hezekiah, who reigned over Judah. Judah was the southern part of the nation of Israel before the kingdom was divided. That's a whole other story!

King Ahaz

King Ahaz came to the throne at age 20 and ruled Judah for sixteen years between 735–715 B.C. He was primarily remembered for his apostasy. The height of his apostasy was making of human sacrifices to heathen gods and his ultimate trust in Assyria when faced with a military threat. His actions consequently led to divine judgment upon Judah.

The name Ahaz is a shortened form of Ahaziah or Jehoahaz, with an element expressing God's name, "iah" and "Jeho", omitted. Thus his name means WITHOUT GOD. How prophetic! The accounts of King Ahaz are found in 2 Kings 16; 2 Chronicles 28, and Isaiah 7. The common theme about King Ahaz is that was one of the most evil and vilest rulers of the southern kingdom of Judah. He was succeeded by his son, King Hezekiah. (See 2 Kings 18).

Unlike his father King David, Ahaz was one king who did not do what was right and pleasing to God. He was a person of his own mind and not after the heart of God like David. He was quick to turn to the ways of the kings of their twin brother nation, Israel. He was heavily idolatrous with no one in the history of the kings to break his record. He probably sacrificed his own sons as burnt offering to heathen demon gods. In short, he did not win any Father of the Year awards during his reign.

He replicated the acts and practices of the Canaanites, Hivites, and Amorites that God had driven out the land. He built high places or altars to idols and made sacrifices on them under trees. He completely loitered the land with abominable blood.

When Rezin, king of Syria, and Pekah the son of Remaliah, king of Israel came to battle against him, King Ahaz, sought help from the King of Assyria and not from the Lord God of Israel. He sent messengers to Tiglath-pileser, the king of Assyria, saying, *"I am your servant and your son. Come up and rescue me from the hand of the king of Syria and from the hand of the king of Israel, who are attacking Him."* 2 Kings 16:7 (NIV). Then he did the worst; he mortgaged his life with the vessels consecrated for the service of the Lord in the temple by sending them as present to the King of Assyria in exchange for help. He desecrated the items specifically reserved for the worship of God.

As if that was not enough, King Ahaz then went to visit the King of Assyria who had agreed to help him. He saw a heathen altar that he felt was better than the one for the God of Israel. He sent the model of that altar to Urijah the priest in Judea and instructed him to build an altar to Jehovah exactly like the model.

Ahaz removed the altar of the Lord from its place in the temple. He then ordered all the offerings and sacrifices to the Lord, as had been commanded by His servant Moses, to be made at certain designated times, to now be made on the strange new altar to the gods and demons behind that altar. This was a complete defiance on the holiness of the God of Israel.

To add to his many sins and just to please the king of Assyria instead of the God of Israel, he removed the canopy cover that had been constructed inside the palace for use on the Sabbath day, as well as the king's outer entrance to the Temple of the LORD. This was a complete desecration of the Sabbath of the Lord which was to be holy to the Lord. He did this just to find favor with a heathen king so that the king would help him fight against Syria and Israel.

In the account of his life that we have reviewed, we see King Ahaz's blatant lack of a trust in the God of Israel, the God of his fathers. When he appealed to Tiglath-pileser III, the Assyrian king, for help, the wrath of the prophet Isaiah came upon Ahaz. The ensuing encounter between the two of them is captured in Isaiah chapter 7 and led to Isaiah's prediction of the birth of Immanuel as a sign of the dissolution of the countries of Israel and Syria. True to God's Word from the mouth of the prophet Isaiah, those two kingdoms were ultimately destroyed by Tiglath-pileser in a campaign that lasted about two years.

It is evident that Ahaz's lack of trust in God seemed to have stemmed from his complete rejection of the Mosaic or traditional Jewish faith rather than from the dangerous political situation.

King Ahaz took the nation of Judah into total ruin, and it was this legacy that his son, Hezekiah, inherited. King Hezekiah attempted to reverse his father's political and religious policies.

King Hezekiah

The name Hezekiah is derived from the combination of the verbal root "chazaq" which means "to strengthen and the shortened form "yah" of the divine name Yahweh, which means "the Lord strengthens." Hezekiah was the 13th king of Judah for 29 years between 726 and 697 BC during which time the northern kingdom of Israel fell to the Assyrians, and Judah itself was invaded by the Assyrians. He is remembered for his religious reforms, for breaking allegiance with Assyria in favor of an alliance with Egypt, and for his illness and miraculous recovery.

Hezekiah's Religious Reforms

Hezekiah came to the throne at a critical juncture in Judah's history. Judah was militarily weakened from wars and raids by surrounding nations during the reign of Ahaz. Perhaps motivated by warnings to the northern kingdom delivered by the prophets Amos and Hosea that punishment would come if Israel did not turn back to God, Hezekiah began his religious reforms soon after becoming king.

In the first month of his reign, Hezekiah opened the temple doors and repaired them. He brought the Levites together and ordered them to "sanctify" themselves and the temple, and to reinstate the religious ceremonies that had long been neglected. Hezekiah restored sacrifices and the priestly temple service.

Hezekiah then sent invitations throughout Judah and Israel for the people to come to the Passover celebration in Jerusalem. It was hoped that religious unification would be a prelude to a political reunification of the two kingdoms - the northern kingdom of Israel and the southern kingdom of Judah. However, Israel ridiculed the Judean messengers who brought the invitations, and only a few persons from the tribes of Asher, Manasseh, and Zebulun went to Jerusalem for the celebration.

After the Passover observance, the worshippers set about destroying the high places and altars. They broke the pillars and cut down the Asherim throughout Judah, Benjamin, Ephraim, and Manasseh. Hezekiah smashed the bronze serpent that Moses had made for it had become an object of worship and identified with a serpent deity, Nehushtan. Because of Hezekiah's sweeping reforms, later generations said of Him: "there was none like him among all the kings of Judah after him, nor among those who were before him." (2 Kings 18:5)

As seen in the story of Gideon and the Nation of Israel, redemption is always available for those who turn their hearts back to God. And we can undo the sins of our fathers in the natural and spiritual realms.

Hezekiah is an example of a son who took a stand regarding his past and created and new future and destiny. The same can be for you. Your upbringing does not define you. You are not defined by the words or curses spoken over you by your elders. You are not bound to repeat the mistakes your parents may have made. In Christ, you are a new creation.

A New Beginning

"In the first year of his reign, in the first month, he opened the doors of the house of the Lord and repaired them. He brought in the priests and Levites and assembled them in the square on the east and said to them, 'Here me, Levites. Now consecrate yourselves and consecrate the house of the Lord, the God of your fathers and carry out the filth from the holy place, for our fathers have been unfaithful and have dealt with evil in the sight of our Lord, our God.

They have forsaken him and have turned away their faces from the habitation of the Lord and turned their backs. They have also shut the doors of the vestibule and put out the lamps and have not burned incense or offered burnt offerings in the holy place to the God of Israel. Therefore, the wrath of the Lord came upon Judah and Jerusalem and he has made them an object of horror, of astonishment and of hissing, and as you can see with your own eyes, for behold, our fathers have fallen by the sword, and our sons and daughters and our wives are in captivity for this.'"

"For it is now in my heart to make a covenant with the Lord, the God of Israel, in order that his fierce anger may turn away from us. My sons, do not now be negligent, for the Lord has chosen you to stand in his presence, to minister to him and be his ministers and make offerings to him."

"And they gathered their brothers and consecrated themselves and went in as the king commanded, by the words of the Lord, to cleanse the house of the Lord, and the priests went into the inner part of the house of the Lord to cleanse it and they brought out all the uncleanliness that they had fun in the temple of the Lord into the court of the house of the Lord, and the Levites took it and carried it out to the brook Kidron. They began to consecrate on the first day of the month, and on the eighth day of the month they came to the vestibule of the Lord. Then for eight days they consecrated the house of the Lord, and on the sixteenth day of the first month, they finished. They went to Hezekiah, the king, and said 'We have cleansed all the house of the Lord, the altar of burnt offering and all its

utensils and the table for the bread and its utensils and all the utensils that King Ahaz discarded in his reign when he was faithless we have made ready and consecrated, and behold, they are before the altar of the Lord."
2 Chronicles 29:3-19 (ESV)

Undoubtedly, Hezekiah cleaned his room, in this case, the temple of the Lord. *"But don't you know that your body is the temple of the Holy Spirit."* Please realize that when we talk about *"cleaning your room,"* we are talking about the temple and room of our body. According to the Scripture, your body is a temple and that for the Lord. Specifically, your body is a temple for the Lord Jesus Christ Himself, through the Holy Spirit. Thus, I want you to see the parallel between Hezekiah's temple in Jerusalem and your body as the temple of the Holy Spirit.

Cleanse the Temple

From the Scripture, we see the first action that Hezekiah took was to cleanse the temple. Let us look at the life, work and reign of Hezekiah before he became king. Hezekiah had an infamous father, King Ahaz, a horrible role model who ruled for about 16 years. If we read 2 Chronicles 28, we would see a small picture of life with Ahaz. The Scripture says that *"Ahaz was 20 years old when he began to reign, and he reigned for 16 years in Jerusalem. But he did not do what was right in the eyes of the Lord as his father had done. He walked in the ways of the king of Israel. He even made metal images for the balls and made offerings in the Valley of the Son of Hinnom where he burned his sons as an offering to idols according to the abominations of the nations whom the Lord drove out before the people of Israel. Ahaz sacrificed and made offerings on the high places and the hills and under every tree."*

Hezekiah saw all of this. His father, his role model, was grossly sinning against the Lord. Ahaz defiled the temple by adding things that did not belong there. 2 Chronicles 29:6 says that *"our fathers have been unfaithful and have done what was evil in the sight of the Lord, our God. They have forsaken him and have turned away their faces from the habitation of the Lord and turned his back."*

Ahaz was not a good role model. Ultimately, Hezekiah had to deal with his dad's mess and past inheritances. This is what we call a generational sin. Hezekiah had to deal with his father's sin. Well, that doesn't seem very fair but if we look at sin, we see that every sin has a consequence.

We know that God is just and merciful. And because He is just, He requires a consequence for every sin. We know from Scriptures that the wages of sin is death Romans 6:23. That means there's always a consequence for sin. But thanks be to God that we're justified when we believe in Jesus Christ and the sacrifice He made on the Cross. We are justified by faith so that God views our sin as if it had not happened.

INIQUITY

There is a consequence called iniquity, a fancy Bible term. Iniquity is a leaning or tendency towards sin. When Adam and Eve committed the first sin, they didn't die physically but there was a consequence of their disobedience. They were shut out of the Garden of Eden. Thus, the consequence of sin was a separation between them and God. This iniquity traveled down through generations. You hear the story of Cain, Abel, anger, and the fall. That's the iniquity that gets passed on from one generation to the next.

In Exodus 20 verse 5, the Scripture says that God *"visits the iniquity of the fathers upon the children to the third and fourth generation."* We all have this iniquity. Although we've been justified, and the sin has been forgiven and forgotten, we go through a process of sanctification. That's where God's mercy comes in. He wants us to grow to be more like Him. Jesus was perfect. We are not. We are going to have tendencies toward sin and we're also going to have a tendency towards iniquity, the sin of our fathers.

Let me explain it this way: Jesus said in the Sermon on the Mount that if you lust after a woman, you have committed adultery. That means that adultery is a sin and there is an ultimate consequence of it. Lust, the tendency to gaze and to look with inordinate affection, is also an iniquity. So one can receive forgiveness and justification from the sin of adultery when he repents and takes Jesus as His Lord and Savior. The iniquity that brought about the adultery would not have been dealt with except through the sanctification in the process of time.

How many of you said, "I am never going to be like my mom and dad"? You said, "They're always arguing." Or, "They're always doing this. I'm never going to do that!" So you get married and you have kids, and they do something wrong. They didn"t clean their room and you start getting angry. You start yelling at them and all of a sudden, you sound just like your mom and dad. That's iniquity. That's the consequence of sin that we are talking about here and that we are all dealing with.

Hezekiah said in verse 9, *"For behold, our fathers have fallen by the sword, they have committed the sin and our sons and daughters are in captivity because of this."*

At this point, you might say, "Great! This is a good pick-me-up message. Now I have to deal with all the stuff in my past." But the good news is you can deal with all the stuff in your past. Just look at what Hezekiah did. He put a stop to the generational sin that his father before him had committed. We can halt iniquity. We can clean our rooms. But here's what we need to do first.

FACE IT

The Scripture says: *"The first year of his (Hezekiah's) reign, in the first month, he opened the doors of the house of the Lord and he repaired them."* The first month in the first year, Hezekiah took action. He didn't say, "Well, I'll do it when I kind of feel like it," or, "Well, re-election time is coming up. So maybe I should do a whole bunch of stuff to make everyone like me." He didn't wait for when the time seemed just right and he felt perfect. No. He took action immediately. He took action in the very first month of his reign. He did not delay. He saw the issue and he faced it head on. He dealt with it.

OPEN THE DOORS

When someone comes to your front door and you don't know who the person is you kind of open up and just peek out. You don't open the door all the way. How many times have we done this? We open the door and say, "Well, I apologize. My house is a mess." We say this sometimes even when our house seems to be looking good. But we need to open the doors and we need to face the stuff that we're dealing with. We can't hide it anymore because hiding it and shoving it under the sofa for so long has been causing that iniquity to continue, that tendency to sin over and over and over again. We've got to open the doors and we have to face it.

It's not going to be pretty. There's some stuff in there, in our temple, that we've pushed aside and pushed back because they are things we don't want to deal with. We put it back around the corner where hopefully no one will see it. We have a pile over here and hopefully people won't see that. So everything looks perfect from the front entryway. But do not go in that back bedroom; it's messy in there. We need to open the doors and we need to face it.

REPAIR THE DOORS

Hezekiah repaired the doors. Wouldn't it be ridiculous to have a safe with rusty hinges and a lock that does not function when all of your prized possessions are kept in this safe? Why would you have everything that you value and treasure in this safe with doors that are insecure?

The doors symbolize a gateway. It is through the gateway of our soul that we allow things to get in and add to our clutter. We know that our soul has many gateways - the eye gate, the ear gate, the mouth gate, the nose gate and the touch gate just to mention but a few. So negative influences can come in by way of what we watch on television, through the eye gate, and may have a significant impact on us. If we don't repair the doors, if we don't fix the gateway to our heart, mind, and soul, whether it be through the eye, ear, nose and any of the other gate, then we're doing ourselves a disservice.

We need to repair the gates. Take the doors off, repair them, and coat them with gold, which symbolizes God, His mercy, and His grace laid upon those doors. We need to open them up. We need to face whatever is in there. We've got to fix the doors to our hearts and our souls because, regardless of what happens next, we don't want the iniquity to come back in and affect us.

A Place of Worship

Don't forget that it is going to get messy as we clean our temple and repair the doors. There are some things in there that we do not want to deal with, to be honest with ourselves about. We still have to prepare ourselves.

The Scripture again says in 2 Chronicles 29:4, that *"He (Hezekiah) brought the priests and the Levites and assembled them in the square."* Back then, it was the job of the priests and the Levites to usher people into worship. It was their job to help bring the Word to life for them to help bring the people to God. When you're preparing to open the doors and to clean your room, you need to get into a place of worship where there is stillness. You need to be with God. You need to invite Him in. You need to have some worship music playing so you can feel the Holy Spirit moving. You need to make a habit of just sitting back and soaking in His presence.

Sometimes we can be dealing with some unpleasant stuff, so we are going to need some people with us. You will need some trusted advisors. You will need some accountability partners. You need your pastor and your life group leaders to help walk you through some of the stuff that you'll be facing because you can't do this by yourself. You've got a body of people who love you and care for you. They want you to be whole.

They're the ones you need to involve in this cleaning of your room. You need to have people who are there to pray with you as the Holy Spirit guides you through this process. Proverbs 24:6 says: *"for by wise guidance you can wage your war, and in abundance of counselors there is victory."* (ESV)

THE INNER ROOMS

In verse 16 of the same Scripture, the Bible says: *"The priests went into the inner part of the house of the Lord to cleanse it and they brought out all the uncleanliness they had found in the temple of the Lord into the court of the house of the Lord. The Levites took the unclean stuff and carried it to the Kidron Valley."* In other words, they went into the inner part like you have to go back into that corner where you piled up everything that no one else can see it. That stuff, you know! Not the very obvious stuff. They went like you must go, deep.

Like Hezekiah, you need to go back to your childhood and deal with things that were said or done to you when you were three, four, or five years old. Some things in your past go back generations. Some things happened and we may not know exactly what's back there. Nevertheless, we need to bring those things out. Those are the things that we need to bring forward. We need to deal with them.

The priests didn't go into the inner part of the Lord's temple and bring out just the light stuff, the stuff that was easy to carry, or the stuff that didn't matter. No! They went in and they brought out all of the uncleanliness. Everything!

I mean everything - all of the issues, the useless, the bad, and the ugly. They took it all. They picked it up. They got that sin that they were dealing with over and over and over again, and they got rid of it and everything.

WORLDLY CORRUPTION BRINGS SPIRITUAL RUIN

Ahaz worshiped foreign gods thinking they would strengthen him. Instead, they were his ruin. Corrupting influences of the world will result in spiritual ruin. I see the story of Ahaz today in the church and the ground on which it is treading now. We hear preachers and spirit-filled people warning the church concerning worldliness and we do not seem to be paying attention to that warning.

We cannot mess with the world and its corrupting influences and end up in spiritual decadence. We do not have to look to Satan and ask for his power to do the work of the ministry, which ultimately is the work of God. I have heard and know of many self-proclaimed supposed gospel preachers who in the craze for power give room to the occult, seeking help from the enemy. There have been false prophets reciting words from psychics and passing it off as the word of God.

This is ruining our call and work and will ultimately bring the judgment of God. The question is whether we are gospel workers, just believers in Christ, or professors of Jesus as the Son of God. We should shun the corrupting influences of the world. Their ultimate end is spiritual ruin. It is a downward movement into the gates of hell itself. We cannot love the world and love God equally.

REFUSE THE THREATS OF THE ENEMY

We see from the story and life of King Hezekiah that we do not need to be afraid of the threats of the enemy; he is just a toothless bulldog. All he wants to create in us with all his threats is fear, which ultimately brings our downfall. I think that might account for why God, in every of His encounters in the Bible with us, would say first and foremost: **fear not**.

We see Hezekiah took the threats of the enemy to the Lord (2 Kings 19:14) What do you do with the threats that Satan brings against you? Do what Hezekiah did, take them to the Lord.

God told Hezekiah there was no need to fear for the enemy would be removed from the land. True to God's Word, it happened as the Lord said. And just as God defeated the Assyrians, He has defeated Satan. So you need not fear his threats. This is the word of the Lord!

It's a process

You and I need to face everything that is cluttering our room. We need to take responsibility. Yes, the Holy Spirit and the people praying for you are going to guide you through the cleansing process. But you need first and foremost to own up to it and take responsibility. As you are cleaning, you cannot and must not allow anything to remain.

In verse 17, the Scripture says: *"They began to consecrate on the first day of the first month, and on the eighth day of the month, they came to the vestibule of the Lord, and then for eight days they consecrated the house of the Lord, and on the sixteenth day, of the first month they finished."* That's a process. This was not a one and done type of thing. Your cleaning is going to be an ongoing process. But God is there for you in the long haul.

Partner with the Holy Spirit

Let's talk about something more specific in this cleansing process - consecration. It means to purify. It's a process that we have to go through and it is the Holy Spirit who does it for us, helping us in this process, while we do our part of cooperating with Him. When you prepare yourself and get yourself into that quiet place with the worship music playing and you've got your intercessor right there and you're getting deep, the Holy Spirit is going to reveal to you the areas of your life that you need to deal with. He's going to be there for you. He is your Comforter and your Guide.

The Scripture in John 16:13 say of the Holy Spirit: *"When the spirit of truth has come, he will guide you into all truth"* The Holy Spirit is going to guide you through your cleansing process. He's going to reveal things that will make you say, "Oh, really?" or "That was set upon me?" or "That was done to me?" or "I did that?" or "I need to forgive that person?' or "I need to repent of that sin?" The Holy Spirit is going to guide you through the process of cleansing and consecration. There may have been some tough times in your life that you have pushed way deep into the recesses of your mind. The Holy Spirit is going to be there to guide you, to lift you up and heal very emotional things. He's going to show you God's truth about what happened. It was not your fault and you are not alone in this thing. Hezekiah had to clean up a mess that was not his fault. The Holy Spirit is going to show you what really happened. You have been holding onto ungodly beliefs about what occurred in your past.

The Holy Spirit is going to wrap the love of God around that situation and say, "God was there. He loved you. He still loves you. I'm sorry that happened to you. But God loves you. He sent His Son to die on the cross for you. Whatever happened to you is not your fault. You didn't cause that." The Holy Spirit is going to be there to guide you through this emotional time of cleansing and is going to reveal the true power of God in that situation. And in the process of cleansing, once you see something, once the Holy Spirit reveals it, you need to confess it and let it go.

There is scriptural foundation for the consecration process. In Nehemiah 9:2, the Scripture says, *"They had confessed the iniquities of their fathers and of their own iniquities."* We too need to do that and then apply the blood of Jesus shed on the cross for our sins, for our family, and for our generation. We can't control what others did, but we can do something about it. Hezekiah could not control what his father did but he could take a stand against it. He could say, "You know what? I cancel what was done before. Through the power of Jesus Christ, whatever my father did is done. Whatever my grandfather did to cause this iniquity in my life is done. I confess it in the name of Jesus. I put it on the cross; I apply the blood of Jesus upon it, and it is done. It's forgiven and it's forgotten." We need to take a stand for the generations in our past and cancel the sin. Cancel that iniquity in the name of Jesus Christ.

The Little Skunk

If there is something that you're dealing with that the Holy Spirit brought to mind, you have to confess that. It is like a skunk that comes in a room, does its business and is gone. The "sin" happened. The skunk stunk. The skunk is gone, but what remains? The stink. The skunk stunk. The smell is still there. It's an offensive odor and it doesn't go away instantly just because the skunk has left the building. There is a residual foul odor residing there long after the skunk has gone away.

The same is true if we have this habitual sin we keep coming back to. Although we confessed the sin and it's forgiven and forgotten, we still have to deal with the stench. We have to turn away from the stench.

Here's what you need to do: say to yourself, "I don't want to go that way. The power of Jesus and His sacrifice on the cross made that way dead to me. I'm going to go this other way." Although this way may seem hard at first because it is unchartered territory with no recognizable trail and we don't know where we need to go, we have to start hacking away and very soon we will start blazing this new trail. Yes, this is a new trail; a new thought process for our minds. This is a renewed mind. And as we focus on this newness of life, that old path no longer beckons to us. The old path, the iniquity, will go away because we have a new focus and the new thoughts, habits, and actions will grow.

We have to start changing our thoughts. We have to reprogram our mind with "I don't want to go this way anymore." I know it is not going to be easy, it is going to take some work, and that it is going to be a process. When we start walking this way, we are going to be able to walk away from those past tendencies in time. So don't give up. Yes, it is going to be hard. It's a process. But there is a God who loves you and there are people who love you.

THE PROMISED LAND

We know that Hezekiah would not have had to deal with his father's sins if the nation of Israel had only listened to what God told them to do when they walked into the Promised Land. In Numbers 33:52, 55 (NKJV) God says, *"'...you shall drive out all the inhabitants of the land from before you, destroy all their engraved stones, destroy all their molded images, and demolish all their high places...' But if you do not drive out the inhabitants of the land from before you, then it shall be that those whom you let remain shall be irritants in your eyes and thorns in your sides, and they shall harass you in the land where you dwell."*

Israel went into the Promised Land with that instruction, and they were supposed to get rid of everything in the land. They were expected to get rid of all the idols and all the nasty stuff. They were expected to get rid of all the sin that was left there. But they did not get rid of it all. They didn't do what God had told them to do. Today, you and I need to go in and drive out the inhabitants of our promised land. We need to go in, take our promised land, and not have anything ungodly remain there.

We only need to do what God has called us to do. We have an opportunity right now to stop the iniquity. All the stuff that has been in our lives, in our past, we can stop right now. All those anger issues? It stops with you. All that pride and arrogance! It stops with you. All that attraction to lust and addictions! It stops with you, now and not tomorrow. Not next week. Not a month from now. Now! *"In the first week of the first month of the first year,"* We must deal with it now.

FREEDOM

Perhaps some things have come to your mind, things that you've been dealing with. Maybe thoughts have been going over and over in your head, thoughts like, "Why do I keep on doing this?" or "Why do I keep on having these thoughts?" or "Why do I keep on doing this and that?" or "Why do I keep on returning to that sin?" I want an opportunity for you to clean the house. I believe you are ready. I want you to believe that Jesus, through the sacrifice that He made on the cross for you and me, can break the power of iniquity. Right here! Right now!

I am going to lead you in a prayer. I want you to believe in your heart that Jesus' blood was shed for you. It was shed for that iniquity you find yourself dealing with. It was shed in order for you to be free. Jesus went to the cross. He carried the iniquities of us all. We come to Him and confess that He is the Lord of our lives, and that He shed His blood for us. So if you're dealing with lust, if you're dealing with anger, if you're dealing with pride, if you're dealing with adultery in your past, if you're dealing with sexual sin in your past, you can bring it to the cross right now. If you want to get rid of it, I want you to say, "I want to get rid of this (call it by its name). I want this (name it) to be gone."

Pray this prayer with me now: Father, I come to you in the name of Jesus. I believe right now that Jesus freed me and cleanses me from all iniquity. The blood of Jesus shed on the cross cleanses me from all iniquity. Lord, I confess my sin, this iniquity, right now, in the name of Jesus. I bring it to the cross. I hold the cross in place for my family. I hold the blood of Jesus against that iniquity. I refuse its power. I am dead to that sin in the name of Jesus. Lord, I ask that you obliterate, through the blood of the cross of Christ, every opposing thought that has been holding me captive with this sin.

Lord, I thank you for setting me free, in the matchless name of Jesus. Amen!

CHAPTER TEN - JERICHO

> *"A wise man scales the city of the mighty and brings down the stronghold in which they trust."* Proverbs 21:22 (ESV)

"There was once a tyrant who ordered one of his subjects into his presence, and ordered him to make a chain. The poor blacksmith—that was his occupation—had to go to work and forge the chain. When it was done he brought it into the presence of the tyrant, and he was ordered to take it away and make it twice the length. He brought it again to the tyrant, and again he was ordered to double it. Back he came when he had obeyed the order, and the tyrant looked at it, and then commanded the servants to bind the man hand and foot with the chain he had made and cast him into prison. That is what the devil does with man. He makes them forge their own chain, and then binds them hand and foot with it, and casts them into outer darkness.[1]" From Moody's Anecdotes, pp. 48-49.

Jericho

The city of Jericho is commonly known in Sunday school stories as having a great wall that came tumbling down after the nation of Israel marched around it seven times and blew their trumpets. However, Jericho, based on archeological records had two large stone walls surrounding it, an inner one and an outer one. The outer wall was measured at 6 feet thick and 20 feet high, while the inner one was 12 feet thick and 30 feet high. Between the two walls was a 15-foot walkway on which the guards were positioned. From a military standpoint, Jericho was an impenetrable fortress. When God promised the land where Jericho was to the nation of Israel, this great walled city was the first insurmountable obstacle they had to face before they could take the rest of the Promised Land.

We are going to look at how Jericho represents many things that have been built up in our lives and create a barrier between God and us. From what we have read in the previous chapters, we know we may not be acutely aware of how the enemy is attacking us. Even with this revelation, there will be things we discover, as we grow deeper, with our relationship with God.

There may be some habitual sin, or root of bitterness, or unforgiveness that has been preventing you from going deeper with God. He has too much for you, but maybe you have an old, bad attitude that is hindering you. Whatever it is from your past that the enemy got you to believe is a stronghold. It is a wall - a barrier between you and all that God has for you.

To receive everything that God has for you, you must tear down those strongholds! Let's look at this story of Jericho. There are some key truths in this story that you can apply to your own life and strongholds.

UNDERSTAND YOUR POSITION

> *Now it came about when Joshua was by Jericho, that he lifted up his eyes and looked, and behold, a man was standing opposite him with his sword drawn in his hand, and Joshua went to him and said to him, "Are you for us or for our adversaries?" He said, "No; rather I indeed come now as captain of the host of the LORD." And Joshua fell on his face to the earth, and bowed down, and said to him, "What has my lord to say to his servant?" The captain of the LORD'S host said to Joshua, "Remove your sandals from your feet, for the place where you are standing is holy." And Joshua did so.* Joshua 5:13-15 (NASB)

Joshua started this endeavor by looking up. He wasn't looking at the situation before him. He wasn't focusing on the problem of the massive stone walls. He didn't start complaining to his co-workers about how they were going to tackle this problem. He looked up and had an encounter with God.

When Joshua looked up, he saw someone standing in front of him with a sword in his hand. The person said he was the "captain of the host of the LORD." When someone introduces himself as "the captain of the host of the Lord", I'm pretty sure one should pay attention. Many people have speculated about who this "man" was. Some say it was a "Christophany," a theological term which is the appearance of Christ in the Old Testament. Regardless if this was an angel or Christ Himself, he depicts a great first foundational element to spiritual warfare.

The reason this is so important is what the captain of the Lord's host represents. He is the one who is in control. He is the one who walks in victory. He is armed for battle, signifying that He is the one who is fighting the battle for Israel.

Have you looked up and met Jesus? Do you have a personal relationship with the Lord Jesus Christ? Would you be able to say that He is your Lord and Savior? Do you recall that time in your life when you made the decision to change direction and accept God's grace and mercy? We cannot go and be victorious if we do not have a salvation experience.

Joshua's experience with the Lord caused him to bow down and worship. How's your worship? Is it just reserved for Sunday mornings, or is it an integral part of your walk with God? Experiencing the presence of God will cause you to bow down and worship.

We must acknowledge and understand that when we have a solid walk with God, the victories we have are His; they are not of our own doing. We must realize that we need to surrender every part of our life and trust Him to bring us to victory in every battle we fight. As we grow closer to Him, we need to surrender all aspects of our lives to Him and trust that He will bring us to the place of victory. Is He Lord of all in ALL aspects of your life? Is there anything that you are still trying to control? Surrender it!

When Joshua asked the Lord; *"Are you for us or for them?"* the Lord answered, *"No!"* That's not a straightforward answer. Kind of makes you wonder what he was doing there if He wasn't there for Joshua or Jericho. Why was He there then?

The answer is found in what the Lord instructed Joshua to do in verse 15. *"Remove your sandals from your feet."* Removing one's shoes in the presence of holiness signifies devotion, or reverence, as well as surrender. Joshua was asked to surrender all power and authority of this battle to the Lord.

Joshua at that moment realized that the Lord was the power behind the impending victory that was to come. This is the only way to be victorious - surrendering ourselves completely to Him.

There are some of us today who have been struggling to fight our battles our own way and by our own power. If we continue in this, we will keep getting defeated by the enemy.

We need to turn it over to the Lord and ask Him to help fight these battles. Jesus already paid the price on the cross to become victorious over the enemy. It's time we acknowledge Him as the One who will fight for us. In surrendering, we need to become vulnerable and go to a place where we are completely yielded to God.

If you notice, in the scripture above, Joshua is on his knees, head bowed. The Lord is standing there with a sword in His hand. This depicts complete surrender. We need to do the same.

God's Promise

Joshua was already walking into this situation based on God's promise. But as he encountered the Lord, he had to be reminded again that Jericho was going fall, and Israel would be victorious. God had already promised the nation of Israel the Promised Land over 40 years earlier. Sometimes we need to be reminded of God's word.

As you look at your life right now, over the strongholds that the enemy has constructed, you might be wondering if you will ever have victory over them. Yes, you can. I sure did.

We need to pray, so we do not forget that our God keeps His promises. He has promised us the victory, and sure enough and true to His promise, the victory shall be ours. *"But thanks be to God! He gives us the victory through our Lord Jesus Christ"* 1 Corinthians 15:57 (NIV).

Please do not forget that whatever God has promised, He is more than able to bring it to pass in our lives. Let us face our strongholds with the assurance that God will do everything He said He would do according to His word.

GOD-FIDENCE

If you will recall, all Joshua was told to do was to walk around the walls. He wasn't instructed to build an arsenal to take down the walls. All the nation of Israel had to do was to follow God's plan, and the walls would "come tumbling down."

God's plan involved "seven priests should bear seven trumpets" and the walk in front of the ark. The priests would blow the trumpets while the people were to walk behind the ark. They were to walk around the city once each day for six days. Then on the last and seventh day, they were to walk around the city seven times and on the seventh round, they were to shout!

Let's look at this in more detail to appreciate the plan that God provided and how we should always trust His word.

SEVEN PRIESTS

The number seven in the Bible stands for completeness or fullness. When priests are mentioned in the Bible, they are presented as representatives of people before God. They stand in the gap, our advocate between God and us. We have the same Advocate in our Lord Jesus Christ.

> "... *we have an advocate with the Father—Jesus Christ, the Righteous One"* 1 John 2:1 (NIV).

As we engage in battle, we must remember that we have a High Priest, one who stands at the right hand of the throne of God, making intercession for us.

The ram or lamb in the Scripture signifies atonement. When Abraham took Isaac to the top of the mountain to be offered as a sacrifice to God, it was a ram that eventually provided the atonement. Atonement is reconciliation with God. This was accomplished by the redeeming work of Christ on the cross.

Only when we receive God's plan of salvation through the shed blood of Christ, are we given the power to enjoy victory over sin and freedom from its power in our lives.

The priests carried the Ark of the Covenant as the Israelites circled the city. We will dive into more details in the next section of this book, but for now, the ark carried the presence of God. Jesus has all power and authority in heaven and on earth, but He also gave that power and authority to us, through Him. We carry the presence of God with us.

The nation of Israel needed to have trust, faith and confidence in God's plan, and follow as instructed they would be victorious. God wanted them to do a simple thing. They needed to walk by faith.

How do you enjoy victory over the strongholds in your life? You yield yourself to His plan. You allow Jesus to live through you and through that you will enjoy His victory.

God wants us to stop trying to fight and win the battles over the strongholds in our lives by ourselves. We need to rest in Him who has already won the victory. All of our efforts and struggles will not gain us victory; only trusting in the power of God will.

When we live in step and in tune with God, it is so freeing. In Him, He is the perfect Advocate. In Him, is the perfect Atonement. In Him, we discover that "It is finished." If we learn to walk in what Jesus has already accomplished for us, then we will reap the victories already won for us.

Conquest

Up to this point, we've been talking about the preparation for taking Jericho, and correspondingly, the preparation for the battles against the strongholds in our lives. Let us focus now on the actual conquest and victory.

In Joshua 6:6-21, we read of the victory Israel achieved through God at Jericho. They followed God's instructions and God's promise was delivered concerning victory.

I've always wondered what the nation of Israel thought when they were instructed just to walk around the walled city. They could have tried to take Jericho by force, but instead, they did it God's way. We will always win, we will always have victory, when we do it God's way.

There is a lot of symbolism in numbers in the Bible. The number six stands for the number of man. I think God was helping the nation of Israel understand that victory wasn't going to come their way. That's why on the seventh day, they walked around Jericho seven times. What happened when the Israelites marched around that city for the seventh time, on the seventh day and then end it with a shout? The walls fell!

Victory over our strongholds is achieved when we come to the place where we completely stop trying to get the victory with our hands and put the efforts in God's hands alone! As we move away from the power of our ability and move into the realm of what God can do in our lives, we can and will see all of what God can bring to pass in our lives.

Pulling and Casting Down

The goal of Israel walking around the walled city was to allow God to move and tear down the walls. We partner with God when we pull and cast down the strongholds of the enemy in our lives.

"For the weapons of our warfare are not carnal, but mighty through God, to the **PULLING DOWN OF STRONG HOLDS; CASTING DOWN** *imaginations and every high thing that exalteth itself against the knowledge of God, and bringing into captivity every thought to the obedience of Christ."* 2 Corinthians 10:4-5 (*emphasis mine*)

To "pull down" means to "take down by effort or force[2]." To "cast" means "to throw or hurl[3]." In Romans 13:12 we are instructed to "cast off the works of darkness" and in Matthew 10:8 to "cast out demon powers."

When you pull and cast down strongholds of the enemy, you are waging offensive warfare. We do not need to wait to defend against an attack from the enemy. We are to attack strongholds of the enemy's power.

Walls of Defense

While the primary focus of this chapter is on tearing down the walls, strongholds, in our lives, walls can be used for defense as well. The walls that surrounded Israeli cities were essential for defense. The walls were typically 30 feet high and 10 feet thick. Watchmen were placed on top of the walls to watch for enemy activity. Matthew 5:14 compares the believer to a "city set on a hill". We do need to have our watchmen in our lives, both accountability partners and ourselves, as we are always on guard against the enemy. We need to have spiritual walls of defense against the enemy.

God's Ways Are Not Your Ways

No matter how absurd a situation appears, you must trust God. His thoughts and ways are not like yours (Isaiah 55:8). *"But God chose the foolish things of the world to shame the wise; God chose the weak things of the world to shame the strong."* 1 Corinthians 1:27 (NIV) God intervenes in ways that seem silly to the natural mind. Israel was doing battle God's way, no matter how foolish it appeared.

Seek God's presence

The ark of the Lord, mentioned nine times in verses 6-13, symbolized to Israel that God was with them. The biblical truth contained in the ark of the Lord is amazing. That is why there is an entire chapter in this book about hosting the presence of God in your life. The key takeaway from this battle is this: before entering battle, seek God's presence.

Silence

Israel was told to march in silence, except the sounding of trumpets as they marched around Jericho. They were not to make any sound until they heard the command to shout (v. 10). As parents the value of instilling this strategy in our kids is vital. All kidding aside, the strategy of silence should be used in warfare. We need to be still as we seek God's presence. We need to listen and receive direction from God of when and what to speak.

You shall not pass

The moment the wall of Jericho gave way, the Israelites marched into the city and killed every living thing, human and animal, except for Rahab and her family. That doesn't sound very spiritual but God knew something that applies in our life spiritually. If the people of Jericho were allowed to live, they would ultimately turn the hearts of the Israelites from the worship of the true God to the worship of other gods.. Unfortunately, we see the Israelites in later years failing in this department, causing all sorts of enemies, strongholds, demonic practices, etc. to rise.

It is our responsibility to make sure that once we identify the strongholds in our lives we make sure we close the door on them, with God's power, and not allow them to return. We must eradicate the stronghold completely and leave nothing behind.

There are some strongholds we can defeat today, but if we do not completely eradicate them from the root, they will rebuild themselves in our lives. And the next time it surfaces, it will be stronger than ever and harder to bring down!

What is that stronghold, that lie, from the enemy you believe, that is stopping you from going forward and upwards with God? Is it lust? Is it hatred? Is it envy? Could it be unforgiveness? Or maybe it is bitterness and a critical spirit? Whatever it is, that thing, that stronghold, need not live another day; it has to be conquered right now. You have to bring it to the Lord and then deal and defeat it His way and only His way!

If you are one who has been trying so hard to conquer your strongholds and gain the victory over them without success, come to Jesus now and say, "Lord, I can't do it, but You can." He will change your life. He will enable you to live a life of victory, which glorifies Him.

> *"For though we live in the world, we do not wage war as the world does. The weapons we fight with are not the weapons of the world. On the contrary, they have divine power to demolish strongholds. We demolish arguments and every pretension that sets itself up against the knowledge of God, and we take captive every thought to make it obedient to Christ."* 2 Corinthians 10:3-6 (NIV).

CHAPTER ELEVEN - AMALEK

In the armed services, even non-combat soldiers, such as radio technicians, have to be prepared for actual combat. In some cases, they are trained as part of the base's defense force. During the periodic 'war games' meant to teach the men how to defend the base adequately. A typical assignment may be to guard the end of the runway in the event of an "enemy" or "terrorist" attack. Imagine being one of those guards with only the standard issue rifle with which to do the job.

You might think that guarding the runway with a single rifle would be highly ineffectual. Had there been real invaders or terrorists you may have done your best. But with only one person with a rifle, standing out in the open you probably wouldn't have stood a chance.

Think of having to do these exercises in a non-wartime environment. No expectation of a real attack. No 9/11 had occurred. An attack on American soil wasn't even a consideration. You probably wouldn't have taken those role-plays very seriously. When you don't expect an enemy to attack, you don't bother taking the precautions that might be necessary.

Too often we forget about the enemy that is out to destroy our souls. We don't expect him to attack. Perhaps we feel secure in our good works — we go to church now and then, try to treat everyone well, give to charities; even read our Bibles occasionally. We are like that soldier, alone on that airstrip with a small weapon and, unfortunately, when the enemy strikes, we will be defeated before the 'game' has hardly begun.

The Bible says that our enemy *"prowls around like a roaring lion, seeking someone to devour. Resist him, firm in your faith..."* 1 Peter 5:8-9 (ESV).

ATTACK AFTER VICTORY

I know that my experience with an attack after victory is not an exclusive thing. I believe many true believers do experience it. Maybe you have just had a great victory, a major break, a true lifting, a visible manifestation of healing and deliverance but suddenly and unexpectedly while you were still basking in the euphoria of your victory, the enemy struck from behind.

He strikes because you were off guard. He strikes because you have let down your guard because of a present victory. I know you understand what I am saying. I believe you have been there before and might be there now.

Now what are you supposed to do? Lose heart and be angry with God for not guarding your back? Grow weary through complaints and blame? No! The enemy is good at doing his job. He did the same to the children of Israel when they were still celebrating their deliverance from Egypt just a few days before.

Then Amalek came and fought with Israel at Rephidim. So Moses said to Joshua, "Choose for us men, and go out and fight with Amalek.

Tomorrow I will stand on the top of the hill with the staff of God in my hand." So Joshua did as Moses told him, and fought with Amalek, while Moses, Aaron, and Hur went up to the top of the hill. Whenever Moses held up his hand, Israel prevailed, and whenever he lowered his hand, Amalek prevailed. But Moses' hands grew weary, so they took a stone and put it under him, and he sat on it, while Aaron and Hur held up his hands, one on one side, and the other on the other side. So his hands were steady until the going down of the sun. And Joshua overwhelmed Amalek and his people with the sword. Then the LORD said to Moses, "Write this as a memorial in a book and recite it in the ears of Joshua, that I will utterly blot out the memory of Amalek from under heaven." And Moses built an altar and called the name of it, The LORD is my banner, saying, "A hand upon the throne of the LORD! The LORD will have war with Amalek from generation to generation." Exodus 17:8-16 (ESV).

Rephidim

For every battle, whether physical or spiritual, there is always a battleground. The camping place of Israel in the wilderness of Paran following their exodus from Egypt was the battleground. It was Rephidim.

The Scriptures, in Exodus 17:1, lists Rephidim as Israel's stopping place after the wilderness of Sin. The scriptural account in Numbers 33:14, 15, however, specifies that after the wilderness of Sin, the children of Israel camped at Dophkah and Alush then Rephidim before they journeyed on to the Sinai wilderness.

Several incidents occurred at Rephidim during the wilderness travels of Israel. Upon Israel's arrival at Rephidim, the Israelites learned there was no water to drink. The thirsty, disgruntled people complained to Moses. Moses, in response, struck a rock in Horeb with his staff according to the Lord's instruction and water issued forth to satisfy the people. Moses renamed Rephidim Massah, which means testing and

Meribah, which means quarreling because of Israel's doubt of the Lord's presence and provision.

This same Rephidim is the site near which the Israelites led by Joshua engaged the Amalekites in battle. God had a strategy for victory in this battle: as Joshua physically engaged the enemy in battle, Moses was to keep his hands in the air. As long as Moses' hands were in the air, Israel prevailed. Moses did as much as Joshua on in the field but only as much as his strength could keep his hands up.

But wisdom came into play. Hur and Aaron came to help Moses by holding up his hands while he sat upon a rock. Sure enough, Moses was able to hold up his hands all day long, and the Israelites prevailed over the Amalekites. The Amalekites were the "first of the nations" to make war against Israel (See Numbers 24:20).

ORIGIN OF AMALEK

We are first introduced to the Amalekites in the Scripture at Genesis 36:10-12. They are descendants of Esau. Esau was one who did not value his inheritance. He placed no value upon the blessings of God. He was a person who focused on meeting his present need at the expense of spiritual inheritance.

Because of this attitude, Esau traded his inheritance of the right of firstborn for a meal. Being profane, he was accessible spiritually and otherwise and so the enemy was able to get a foothold in him (See Ephesians 4:27). After trading his birthright for just a day's lunch, Satan filled his heart with hatred and bitterness against his brother, Jacob, who now had the blessing. Genesis 27:41-42.

The name Amalek according to the Strong's Exhaustive Concordance of the Old Testament means to "dwell in a valley." It is from the root word "to toil or to remove spirit life," which means loss of spirit life through labor, toil, weariness. This is a great example of how your words can create your reality.

The Amalek People

Let us look at the nature of the Amalek people as Israel's opposing force. We see from scripture and history that they were nomads, or nomadic, which makes them a people that wandered or moved from place to place and were never planted anywhere. They were a people that had no certain dwelling places. The spirit of Cain was at work in their national destiny.

They were people who would never make a commitment. They had no roots or connections. They were not joined to anything or anyone for accountability. They were a people wild and left to themselves, so they carried a bitter hatred for the people of God who walked in blessing. They didn't have a land or territorial dispute with Israel. They just hated the people of Israel and desired to destroy them because of the blessing traded off by their grandfather years earlier.

No wonder they carried the same spirit of hatred for the seed of God, and his promise! Does that say something to you about people who just hate and resent you for no just cause and who would rather have you dead than to see a snake killed?

Attacking from Behind

Sometimes someone will just hate you although you never did anything to that person. Satan is like that. So what was the reason for this battle between the Israelites and the Amalekites? The answer is found in Deuteronomy 25:17-18. The Scripture says that the Amalekites attacked Israel from the rear, making a cowardly assault upon the "faint and weary" stragglers.

"Remember what Amalek did to you on the way as you came out of Egypt, how he attacked you on the way when you were faint and weary,

and cut off your tail, those who were lagging behind you, and he did not fear God. Therefore when the LORD your God has given you rest from all your enemies around you, in the land that the LORD your God is giving you for an inheritance to possess, you shall blot out the memory of Amalek from under heaven; you shall not forget."

From the Scripture above, we see that Amalek came up from behind the Israelites unexpectedly and with no warning. It was a time when Israel was tired and weary. This, too, is how the enemy attacks.

REAR RANKS

Please note that the people in the rear ranks are people who are furthest from leadership. Does that tell you something about who Satan targets the most? People who are far from God's leadership and want to live their lives in rebellion and independence are most vulnerable to Satan's attacks.

People in the rear ranks are those who have lost their strength and lag behind purposelessly and with no vision. They are the people who have become offended or take count of every offense, are doubtful and full of negative thinking. Any person in that state is at the place where the enemy can launch a successful attack on him or her.

TIRED AND WEARY

We saw above that the presence of fatigue and tiredness are Satan's opportunities for attack. The children of Israel were fatigued, tired, weak; they lacked strength and were shattered emotionally thus making them vulnerable. Satan will work successfully on people who are worn down by life's journey, difficulties, demands, and pressure. These people are weary.

Israel was weak and weary when it was attacked by Amalek but did they fight? Sure they did! And did they win the battle? Yes, they did! But how?

Conquer through Prayer

According to scripture, we see that Israel fought the Amalekites and achieved the victory over them but not by sword alone. There is the place of open combat with an enemy and there is the place of quiet intercession. Israel needed both to win in this battle.

We see Joshua practically and physically engaging the enemy in battle and then we see Moses off the battlefield doing the spiritual backing and supply, both of which lead to triumph. One thing about battle is this: it is not just one tribe or one nation fighting against each other. It is a spiritual battle as well. All battles are both physical and spiritual in the context of the Old Testament as territory was being taken away from the enemy. God being the only true God and God of Israel always proved to be superior through assuring Israel's victory.

Moses knew this and took to the spiritual end of the battle. He knew that victory is first spiritual before it becomes physical. Thus, the action taken by Moses is considered an act of prayer (See Exodus 17:9-11). It expressed an attitude of dependence upon God that affected the outcome of the battle (Exodus 17:11). God likes it when we stop fighting and start resting.

Rod of God

Second, Moses, in addition to praying, gripped "the rod of God" so the battle would be won. The rod of God is a symbol of divine authority (See Exodus 17:9). He knew it took more than physical power to fight; it also required authority. On whose authority are you fighting? On your own or someone other than the Lord's authority?

Goliath came against David in the name and authority of his gods, but David came against him in the name and authority of the Lord of hosts, the God of the armies of Israel and he won (See 1 Samuel 17:45). When you go into battle, you must have a firm hold on your divine authority, which is the name of Jesus. It is necessary that you know who you are in God and the authority He has given you.

Jesus said to the disciples, as well as you His followers, *"All authority in heaven and on earth has been given to me"* Matthew 28:18 (NIV). He also said, *"And these signs will accompany those who believe: In my name they will drive out demons; they will speak in new tongues; they will pick up snakes with their hands; and when they drink deadly poison, it will not hurt them at all; they will place their hands on sick people, and they will get well"* Mark 16:17-18 (NIV).

That victory is for you; that victory is for me. We will dive into this deeper in Part Four of this book.

Spiritual Leadership

Third, we see another strategy in this battle that was another key to their victory. It is obedience to spiritual leadership. Joshua knew that although he was the one to fight the enemy head on, he had to obey the instruction of the spiritual leader God had placed over him. It is fearful and humbling to know that an instruction acted upon by a spiritual figure and head could save us many years of toiling in battle. Joshua knew to do as Moses instructed him (Exodus 17:9-10).

Today, God has placed among us people to whom He has given special abilities to lead. He enables these leaders to give direction so His purposes will be accomplished. We must recognize this and follow these leaders as Joshua did. Otherwise, we will get confused when everyone tries to give direction at the same time.

Take up the offense

Fourth, we see another strategy in this battle between these two nations, i.e., the people had to go out and fight. I once heard this statement at my son's football camps, "the best form of defense is a good offense." That means that victory in spiritual warfare comes not just by defense but also by offense.

We can't win the battles against our foe if all we do is to lounge in a corner fending off Satan's shots at us. We must throw our arrows and bombs at him too. At times, offensive strategies are needed. You are to be aggressive in attacking your enemy.

Seek Assistance

Fifth, in spiritual warfare, there is the need to seek assistance. Israel did this. Moses had assistance in the persons of Aaron and Hur. God, in His wisdom, raises up people, men and women, to assist us in meeting spiritual challenges. There is no stand-alone and fight alone if we are to win in spiritual battles.

Victory in spiritual warfare is a partnership. God assigns a role to everyone in this partnership. He called Joshua to assume the military leadership, while He gave the spiritual leadership to Moses. And to Aaron and Hur, He assigned the roles of an assistant who helped Moses by holding up Moses' hands when he grew weary. That is a partnership that works.

Recall Past Victories

Sixth, we see the strategy of recalling past victories in winning the battles against our assailants. When King Saul interviewed teenage David for his epic battle with Goliath, David recounted to King Saul when he was keeping his father's sheep. He told King Saul about how a lion and a bear came to steal and kill some of the flock but that he had killed the lion and the bear. He said he would also kill Goliath because he was insulting the God of Israel.

Remembering, recalling and recounting past conquests through the power of God gives you renewed vigor to face present opposition. This is why God told Moses to write the story of this battle in a book for a memorial and rehearse it in the ears of Joshua. Joshua was destined to be

Moses' successor. He would lead Israel in the conquest of the Promised Land.

REMAIN VIGILANT

A lot of things will happen to us when we do not remain vigilant and stay on guard against the attacks of the enemy. The Bible is full of examples of men and women, who neglected their defenses and the enemy attacked. Some were great men of Scriptures like Adam, Elijah, Moses, Samson, David, John the Baptist, and Apostle Peter.

Adam, the first created human, given all authority to govern God's creation, took his eyes of God and believed a false promise concocted by the enemy.

Moses, even after being in the full presence of God let his anger get the better of him and ended up not entering the Promised Land.

Samson repetitively disobeyed God's commands to keep him righteous which led to his downfall.

All these men had one time or another in their lives when they were negligent and the enemy struck and dealt them hard blows that left them with fatal wounds.

GET RID OF IT ALL

I want to look just beyond the physical Amaleks and their attacks on Israel, to a spiritual Amalek. The enemy does not have many new tricks up his sleeves since his has old tactics that still work today. Remember, if we do not get rid of the things that God has asked us to get rid of, they can come back and develop into a stronghold.

We see evidence of this the life and behavior of the first king of Israel, Saul. In 1 Samuel 15:1-3, God gave a direct mission to King Saul, through the prophet Samuel, to go utterly destroy the Amalek and their stronghold. God had vowed previously in the time of Moses that He would perpetually fight with the Amalek.

> *"And Samuel said to Saul, "The LORD sent me to anoint you king over his people Israel; now therefore listen to the words of the LORD. Thus says the LORD of hosts, 'I have noted what Amalek did to Israel in opposing them on the way when they came up out of Egypt. Now go and strike Amalek and devote to destruction all that they have. Do not spare them, but kill both man and woman, child and infant, ox and sheep, camel and donkey'"* 1 Samuel 15:1-3 (ESV).

King Saul, instead of completely destroying the stronghold of the Amaleks and everything to the letter as God had instructed him, spared the king of Amalek. The king was the spiritual head of a people and in most barbaric cultures like Amalek, the king was the custodian of the deities, authorities, and powers of the culture. King Saul had forgotten that it was a spiritual battle and not just a physical battle between Israel and the Amaleks.

We need to make sure we overpower everything that attacks us. We cannot allow any footholds given to the enemy to establish strongholds.

PART THREE

THE KINGS

CHAPTER TWELVE - KINGS

Leonidas, King of Sparta, was preparing to make a stand with his Greek troops against the Persian army in 480 B.C. when the Persian envoy arrived. One man from the envoy spoke with Leonidas about the futility of trying to resist the advance of the huge Persian army.

"Our archers are so numerous," said the envoy, "that the flight of their arrows darkens the sun."

"So much the better," replied Leonidas, "for we shall fight them in the shade."

Leonidas made his stand and died with his three hundred troops.

VALIANT KINGS

God is looking for valiant kings, men and women of faith who in Christ Jesus have become kings and priests of the Most High. He is looking for valiant people who will be bold, courageous, and strong in the face of adversity and carry out their God-given responsibilities with courage and determination. Moreso, our nation is desperately in need of valiant people, kings who will fight against fear, never retreating from disheartening or difficult tasks.

God is looking for kings who inspire others to be strong and courageous too. And God is doing this regardless of our faults and flaws; He is calling forth our potential. This Psalm of David in the Scriptures says what God is doing right now: *"For the king trusts in the Lord; through the unfailing love of the Most High he will not be shaken"* Psalm 21:7 (NIV).

What does it mean to be a valiant king?

To be valiant means to be bold, courageous and strong in the face of adversity. It means to carry out responsibilities with courage and determination. And we know that courage begins within, it is an internal-spirit force that battles against fear, never retreating from disheartening or difficult tasks. It, in turn, inspires others.

A king is chief or sovereign of a nation; a man invested with supreme authority over a nation, tribe or country; a monarch; a prince; a ruler. In the New Testament sense, it is everyone who has taken Jesus to be their Lord and Savior whether male or female (See Revelation 5:10).

But let us not lose sight of the fact that these kings have flaws and faults that God is aware of, yet He still chooses to call them, empower them with potential and treat them with respect. That's how much God loves and believes in us.

There are some great examples of kings in the Scripture who God called in spite of their flaws and faults. These men are referenced in the "Hall of Faith" passages in Hebrews 11.

Jepthah, the son of a prostitute, was fearful, felt rejected, and lacked confidence in himself.

Gideon was fearful against his enemies and hid in caves, ultimately leading the nation of Israel into seven years of bondage to the Midians.

Samson was laden with sexual sins and disobeyed God on how to keep himself sanctified.

Moses was a murder, had a hard time controlling his anger, and even questioned his ability to lead his people out of bondage.

Abram or Abraham (Father of Nations) full of fear and doubt on God's ability to deliver on a promise lied on multiple occasions to protect himself and his family.

Peter (Rock) denied knowing his Lord three times.

In spite of the flaws of these men, God still called them and used them because He saw beyond their flaws to the real man within, the Valiant Man. And that is the way He sees us still today.

The Ultimate Example of a Valiant Man

I had pointed out earlier that being valiant means to show courage in the face of opposition, difficulty or pain. Also, there is a need for both physical and moral courage. Physical courage is facing fears or facing the unknown while moral courage is saying and doing what is right. We see all of these characteristics in the life of Jesus, our absolute and ultimate example of a valiant man.

In John 17:4, Jesus introduced the great intercessory chapter with these words: *"I glorified you on earth, having accomplished the work that you gave me to do."* What do you make of that? I believe that that is the voice of valiancy.

Jesus remained loyal and faithful to His God-given purpose. He placed the message and values of the Kingdom of God before all else and in doing so, refused to conform to the expectations of others.

Jesus refused to quit or retaliate in the face of opposition or rejection and even demonstrated courage in the face of pain and death. Even when He was on the cross, He showed compassion to others and forgave those who abused Him.

He honored His mother as He was dying on the cross. His entire life was invested in others. He ultimately gave His life so we could become valiant men and women.

You might say, but that was Jesus. However, the truth is that what God did in Christ, He wants to do the same in us too, for God has called us to follow in the footsteps of Christ. He has also made it possible for us to be like Jesus even in our weaknesses and limitations through the provision of the new birth on the ground of redemption.

This is why Jesus stated in John 1:12-13 (ESV) , *"But to all who did receive him, who believed in his name, he gave the right to become children of God, who were born, not of blood nor of the will of the flesh nor of the will of man, but of God."* In this way, these *"all who did receive and believe Him"* become like Christ the King, valiant and courageous, conquering and conquering.

By this, we can say that inside the heart of every Christian is a valiant man or woman waiting to be released in Christ Jesus. But since this valiancy is rooted in Christ, as shown by His example above, I think it would be well for you to have His life and continued work and be released in and through you.

Here is how we can step into the call to become valiant. Receive what it means to welcome Jesus Christ into your life unconditionally. You must believe what He has done for you and will do in you. Embrace His words. Then give yourself to becoming more like Christ.

Speak the truth in love. Do what is right at all times. Show compassion to others. These and much more were the things Jesus did that marked Him as a valiant achiever.

Don't forget this: God did not send you into this world to start your race. He sent you into this world to finish your race valiantly. So learn from Jesus and continue with what He started, the same way He started it.

CHAPTER THIRTEEN - KINGS & PRIESTS

In the previous chapter, we defined the word "King" in the New Testament sense to include every man and woman that has taken Jesus Christ of Nazareth as their Lord and Savor irrespective of their gender.

The Scripture has more to say about this. In 1 Peter2:5, the Scriptures describes the Christian, male and female, like this: *"You also as living stones are being built up into a spiritual home, a holy priesthood to offer up spiritual sacrifices acceptable to God through Jesus Christ."*

We see the Bible using different picture language to describe our identity. It says we are God's spiritual house, His holy priesthood, and a royal priest. The Scripture further supports this point in Revelation 5:10 when it says that God has made (every believer) Kings and Priests.

We see that what we are talking about here concerns you, whether you are a brother or a sister, as long as you are in Christ. You are a King, every believer-male, and female, and you are a Priest, every believer-male and female, and your utmost design as a King and a Priest is to manifest and release the presence of God to invade your life and environment. In doing this, we are taking our place in royalty and showcasing our identity.

The Scripture puts it this way: *"But thanks be to God, who in Christ always leads us in triumphal procession, and through us spreads the fragrance of the knowledge of him everywhere."* 2 Corinthians 2:14 (ESV). That is why we are here, as royalty, to showcase the presence of God everywhere.

God always causes us to triumph. We know that triumph is synonymous with Kings and means to rule and to have dominion in every place. So we are walking in triumph, conquering and having dominion in life and in doing so, we manifest the "savor" of Christ. We know that it is priestly characteristic to manifest the presence of God in service. As priests we carry the presence of God into every place. We are Kings and Priests of the most high, triumphing and manifesting the divine presence everywhere we go.

The Old Testament is filled with practical examples of kingship and priesthood so much so it would do us good to look into it and learn the truth about ruling, which is the function of Kings, and then also service, which is the function of Priests. But first, we are going to turn our search light onto priesthood and what it entails.

The Old Testament priest offered up sacrifices to God. We know that sacrifices in the Old Testament were of animals and sometimes grains. It was the priest's job to make these animal sacrifices to atone for the sins of the people and grain offerings in thanksgiving and worship of the Lord (See Hebrew 5:1).

ARK OF THE COVENANT

One of the jobs the priests in the Old Testament were responsible for was to bear the Ark of the Covenant, which was the presence of God. The New Testament writer of the book of Hebrews gave us a vivid summary description of the Ark in the following words: "...*the ark of the covenant covered on all sides with gold, in which was a golden jar holding the manna, and Aaron's rod which budded, and the tables of the covenant; and above it were the cherubim of glory overshadowing the mercy seat"* Hebrews 9:3-5 (ESV). In that verse, we see the contents of the Ark: gold, Aaron's rod, the tablets of the covenant, the cherubim of glory and the mercy seat.

The Bible gave us another dimension to the Ark of the Covenant that was truly revealing; it was called the place of meeting with God. God said to Moses in the place of the Ark is where I will meet with you and commune with you (See Exodus 25:22). That is revealing!

In every way, the Ark of the Covenant was a symbol of Jesus Christ. Time and time again, we find that the Old Testament, particularly its rituals and symbols were a foreshadow of New Testament, which finds the fulfillment of the Old Testament in Jesus Christ. I think knowing this would help us accept the truth of the symbolism of the Ark of the Covenant.

Knowing about symbolism and foreshadowing, we see the Ark, a wooden box overlaid with gold. The wood represented Jesus' human nature, and the gold represented His divine nature. The mercy seat symbolized Jesus whom God set forth to be our mercy seat according to Romans 3:25. God put Jesus forward as the propitiation by His blood for us to receive by faith. The pot of manna symbolized Jesus as the bread of life. The Tablets of Covenant symbolized Jesus the Word made flesh. And finally, Aaron's rod symbolized Jesus declared the Son of God by the resurrection from the dead.

So with the understanding of the symbolism of the Ark comes the true revelation. The Ark was the meeting place with God. In Jesus, we have a meeting place with God. It was on the cross, in His atoning sacrifice, that Jesus brought God and lost humanity together by bridging the gap through His flesh. In Jesus, humanity meets with God.

Moreover, from Strong's Exhaustive Concordance of the Bible, we understand what the word "meet" in Exodus 25:22 means "to meet at a stated time, to engage for marriage, and also to make an appointment[1]." Therefore, in Jesus we have made an appointment with God, to meet Him at a time stated for marriage. This all took place in Jesus on the cross.

Again, the Ark is the place of meeting and experiencing God. In Jesus, the presence and the reality of God are manifested. *"For in him all the fullness of God was pleased to dwell."* Colossians 1:19 (ESV)

Priests Carried the Ark

We see from the Scriptures that God directed that the priests alone shall carry the Ark of the Covenant and the Ark must not be carried on any carriage. It must be borne by the priests only and on their shoulders in particular. These were set rules that needed to be followed.

At one point, the Israelites violated the rules. The Scripture says that the priest *"…and they carried the ark of God on a new cart"* 1 Chronicles 13:7-10 (ESV). They carried the ark, but in the wrong way. As a result, when the cart toppled, and Uzza reached out to steady the ark, he died. Although he acted with good intentions, he died because his actions did not honor God or His commands, and he was not a priest whose job was to steward the ark.

Though we carry the presence of God and manifest Him to the world, we must do it the God-ordained way. There is a way to conduct the presence of the Lord such that we don't make a mockery of Him and bring God's judgment on ourselves.

The Scripture also shows us how to carry the Ark in the proper way. It states: *"And the Levites carried the ark of God on their shoulders with the poles, as Moses had commanded according to the word of the LORD"* 1 Chronicles 15:15 (ESV). I believe that you are who are today, the priest of the Most High God, have lessons to learn from these Scriptural passages and patterns.

It was the responsibility of the priests to carry the ark which is the presence of God. It wasn't just one priest. Multiple priests walking together in unity carried the Ark. It is not God's will that we walk with Him in isolation from other believers.

We see from the scripture above that by carrying the Ark on a "new cart," the children of Israel opted for an alternative way to doing God's business. The lesson to be learned here is that there is no substitute for doing God's business God's way. We must follow the already laid down protocol of heaven.

As priests, our primary call is to carry the presence of God into the community. This should make us focus on God because we can only carry unto the world what we experience in private with God.

God's corporate plan for us believers as a royal priesthood is to carry His divine presence into our community, to make Christ known. Let us not forget that this responsibility and duty requires more than one person. It requires a body of individuals in unity carrying the presence of God to the world.

Experience the Presence of God

Priests in the Old Testament knew how to invoke the presence of God. They knew what to do to invoke God's manifest presence. I think that we have much to learn about that so we too know what to do to constantly produce and experience the presence of God.

The Scripture in Leviticus 16:11-14 shows three requirements for the priests must have prepared before they can enter and have an encounter with God. The three core elements are wrapped around three compound words: Blood, Incense, and Fire.

> *"Aaron shall bring and kill the bull of the sin offering for himself and for his household."* Leviticus 16:11 (NIV)

The blood of the bull of the sin offering is symbolic of the blood of Christ shed for us on the cross. Thank God, the blood of Christ was already shed for us.

We come into the presence of God by applying the shed blood of Christ to our sins and failures by faith. We know that sin separates us from God and makes us insensitive to Him (See Isaiah 59:1-2). But we equally know that God's remedy for sin is the blood of Jesus already shed. Our response to that remedy is to repent of our sins, confess our faith in Jesus, believe and take the blood of Christ as free access into God's presence without condemnation (See Hebrews 10:19-20).

> *"...and his hands full of sweet incense beaten small, and bring it within the vail."* Leviticus 16:12 (KJB)

Incense is symbolic of thanksgiving and praise. David wrote in Psalm 100:4 for us to *"come into God's presence with thanksgiving and praise."* This is an eternal priestly order that was passed down to his days. He too knew what it meant to be a king and a priest of God.

In addition to coming into God's presence based on the blood of Christ, we must come with an abundance of gratitude and praise. This praise is our spiritual sacrifice! The psalmist, knowing the truth of this statement, also said that God inhabits the praises of His people. He meant that where there are true praise and worship, the divine presence witnesses to it by showing up. Let us go for it (See Psalm 23:2).

> *"And he shall take a censer full of burning coals of fire from off the altar before the LORD."* Leviticus 16:12

Fire in the Scripture represents God's manifest presence, which is the Holy Ghost. To provoke and to experience God's presence in our lives, we must consciously learn to depend on and to cooperate with the Holy Spirit, who will ignite our heart with passion.

The Scripture makes it clear that it is the Holy Spirit's role to help us in prayer, particularly through the gift of tongues, and to also reveal Christ. When we pray depending on the Holy Spirit, He overshadows us with the glory cloud and manifests Jesus to us in ways that we cannot deny. In Jesus, the fullness of the divine presence dwells.

Manifest the Presence of God

God is everywhere but we need to be able to discern how to experience His personal manifest presence. God is everywhere, and we are always joined spirit to spirit with Him. But to make His presence personal and experience Him, we need to become conscious and aware of His presence.

The presence of God can be consciously cultivated. It starts with peace. Peace is a force, a powerful presence of God. We can cultivate it, create it and live it. It is powerful and able to crush the enemy. With such a powerful weapon of warfare, it would behoove us to learn to be at peace with ourselves and the world around us.

To experience peace, we need to be filled will the full measure of God, which is love. Love is God's atmosphere, the highest of the divine presence. Love surpasses knowledge.

Out of love and peace, joy overflows. When you see a believer who is always joyful, know for sure that he or she is being invaded with the presence of God. The psalmist wrote, *"you will fill me with joy in your presence"* Psalm 16:11 (NIV)

When you are cultivating the presence of God in your life, it becomes an outward expression in your life as well. People will be attracted to that. *"When the crowds heard the Apostle Philip and the signs he performed they all paid close attention to what he said"* Acts 8:6 (NIV). Having peace, love, joy, in your life is a powerful tool for witnessing to others.

As we experience His presence, we can hear Him more clearly. We are not distracted by the hustle and bustle of the world. When we hear His voice, the voice conveys the presence of God. When it comes to you, the presence of God comes with all that God is. It can shake the heaven and the earth. You will not be the same.

We also can encounter God in visions, open eye visions, as well in sleep. His desire is to communicate with you. When you are present with someone, you just don't want to sit together silently. While that can be good, God desires to partner with you so He can reveal His desire to see change through you.

At times, God's presence can be so strong that we might not be able to stand before Him. Oh, how glorious to not be able to do anything because the glory of the Lord is pressed down upon you! All you want to do is worship and soak in His presence.

RELEASE THE PRESENCE OF GOD TO OTHERS

Don't forget that as priests; we are specially ordained by God to carry His presence into our communities, to neighbors and people around us. What good is God's presence if we cannot release it to others? The ultimate purpose of the divine presence is not for us to have and to keep to ourselves in selfishness, but to make God real in our world among our people, making them better. Every manifestation and revelation of God are to make people better.

So how do we accomplish this ultimate purpose of God? I think the basic way is through love. As the Scripture says, *"Walk in love as Christ loved us"* Ephesians 5:2 (ESV).

Practice loving people from your heart. The greatest gift from God is love. When we love people sincerely from our heart and show it in the form of kindness, kind and healing words, and kind actions, we are releasing the presence of God to others. God's love was given to us through the Holy Spirit. What has been poured into our hearts, we must pour out of it.

Minister the gifts of the Spirit to people. All nine gifts of the Spirit are manifestations of the presence of God. When we minister the gifts of the Spirit to any person, we are releasing the presence of God to that person.

Testify about Jesus. God has ordained that His presence is communicated and conveyed to people around us through testimony and witness. When we testify and witness about Christ to people, we are subjecting them to the presence of God.

Invite the Holy Spirit to come into situations. The Holy Spirit is the conveyor of the divine presence in the world today. When we invite Him into a situation or into anybody's life, He answers with the divine presence. We know the Holy Spirit has come when we see His manifestation. We do not see Him; we see His works. Stay sensitive to the Holy Spirit.

Another way to release the presence of the Lord to others is by being conscious and sensitive to the Spirit. He is always moving, communicating and working, so when we stay conscious of Him we can discern when He moves. Therefore, to be able to stay sensitive to Him all the time, we have to be quick to resolve sin, avoid grieving Him through disobedience and stay in a constant place of fasting and prayer. With these, we are keen to His actions, and He can reveal Himself through us to others.

Exercise dominion in prayer. As priests of the Most High, we must learn how to exercise dominion and takeover situations through prayers. The prophet Elijah is a perfect example of this in the Bible. He learned the secret of "thus saith the Lord" thereby exercising authority and dominion that was evident for people to see through the power of prayer. I will discuss more on this topic in a later chapter.

CHAPTER FOURTEEN - FALLEN KINGS

Failure is consistent with human nature, and as long as we live in a body of flesh in this world, at one time or another, we will meet with failure. However, as believers our steps are ordered by the Lord, every time we fail, God lifts us back up. This is consistent with the nature and person of God: He always lifts people up again.

We all fail. We need to admit that. We have to take responsibility and acknowledge it so that, in accordance with God's nature, He can forgive us, lift us up and then we can change.

One of the things we have to watch out for in this matter is pride. It is prideful not to admit our weaknesses and failures. It is pride not to come to God acknowledging our weakness and asking Him for His help. *"Whoever conceals his transgressions will not prosper, but he who confesses and forsakes them will obtain mercy"* Proverbs 28:13 (ESV).

This is a fact that the kings knew and dealt with, in the Scriptures. Humans are prone to failure and failing. The only way to receive freedom is to accept our nature and frame, not to think too highly of ourselves, and to look to God to keep us stable. Then when we fail, acknowledge our frailty and run to God for help and change.

> *"For he knows our frame; he remembers that we are dust."* Psalm 103:14 (NIV)

ORIGIN OF THE BLAME GAME

We have discovered that it is human to fail but it is best to acknowledge the failure and ask God to change us. The problem we have is instead of doing this we tend to blame someone else for our mistakes and failures. Now let us examine where this problem started - Adam.

Adam did what God asked him not to do. Afterward, God came in the cool of the day, called to Adam and asked him three questions:

> *"Where are you?"*
> *"Who told you that you were naked?"*
> *"Did you eat of the fruit of the tree?"*
> Genesis 3:9-11 (ESV)

Then Adam answered:

> *"The woman whom you gave to be with me, she gave me fruit of the tree, and I ate."* Genesis 3:12 (ESV)

This is the worst thing we can do when we fail, play the blame game, to shift responsibility.

In pushing the blame on another, Adam refused to assume responsibility for his failure. The word "blame" means to place the responsibility for a failure or mistake on people or circumstances[1]. That was exactly what Adam did; He blamed Eve, and he blamed God. He pushed and placed the responsibility on Eve and ultimately on God.

Unfortunately, this is still the way kings are today. This is the way our culture is today. We live in a blame culture where people fail to assume responsibility for their actions.

I want to show you some of the consequences of the blame game.

When Adam blamed God and Eve for his failure as some Kings do today, he missed an experience and opportunity to grow. This is a fact of the blame game - every time we fail to accept responsibility for our failures, we miss an experience or the opportunity to grow. Accepting responsibility for failure and acknowledging it before God and man is a rare opportunity to grow, but most of us throw it away. By saying sorry for a wrong you grow beyond that wrong.

When Adam blamed, God stopped talking. When we blame instead of accepting responsibility, God stops talking at least as far as that circumstance is concerned. I believe the reason most of us have a problem hearing the voice of God is because of the irresponsibility called the blame game.

When Adam refused to take responsibility for his failure, he experienced the full consequences of it. I believe if he had assumed responsibility, God would have had another way to exonerate him of the consequences or would have at least worked with him for a quick way out.

Based on the above, we can conclude that although blaming may make us feel better, it does not solve and can never solve the problem. It didn't get Adam anywhere, and it will not get us, Kings, anywhere today. Instead, let us be humble enough to accept responsibility for our failures, acknowledge our weaknesses and God will lift us and change us in His love and grace. For *"God opposes the proud, but gives grace to the humble."* James 4:6 (ESV)

Further, blaming stops our shot on the path to empowerment. We cannot be empowered by the Holy Spirit when we are playing the blame game so what are we supposed to do? Take responsibility to for the failure and grow above the situation.

FAILURES AND MISTAKES ARE CERTAIN

Now, we have come to the point in this study where it must be emphasized that failures and mistakes are certain and that none of us Kings are immune to them. They are certain and should be anticipated. God knows this already which is why He made provision in the redemption for the forgiveness of sins. He gives us opportunities to start all over again. *"Oh, the depth of the riches and wisdom and knowledge of God! How unsearchable are his judgments and how inscrutable his ways!"* Romans 11:33 (ESV) What grace! What love!

The Scripture emphasized this in the Epistle of John when it says *"If we say we have not sinned, we make him a liar, and his word is not in you."* 1 John 1:10 (ESV)

Two things are certain in life: death and failure or mistakes.

This is true because whatever you are good at now, you probably failed at it the first time you tried it. If this is true, then every person fails at some time or the other. We must learn to benefit from the mistakes and failures.

The Bible abounds with people (Kings) who failed at one time or the other. Now let us take a look at some of them:

1. Abraham lied about his wife (See Genesis 20:2)
2. Isaac lied about his wife (See Genesis 26:7)

    3. Jacob deceived his father (See Genesis 27:18-27)
    4. Moses murdered a man (See Exodus 2:11-12)
    5. Rahab was a prostitute (See Joshua 2:1)
    6. Gideon was full of fear (See Judges 6:11)
    7. Barak lacked courage (See Judges 4:6-9)
    8. Samson got involved with Delilah (See Judges 16:4)
    9. Jephthah's mother was a prostitute, and he made a foolish vow. (Judges 11:1, 30-31)

In spite of their mistakes the Holy Spirit still called them "Men of Faith" in Hebrews 11. We can easily say this: God sees people not in the light of their mistakes but in the light of their destiny and their response.

We know that God does not overlook failures, but He does not focus on them. Rather, He imparts grace to us to live on after repenting. So we deceive ourselves if we think we cannot fail. We make God a liar by doing that. But what matters most is how we respond to our mistakes and what we do with our failures? Deal with your mistakes honestly.

There were magnificent failures and obvious mistakes made by great men and women all through the Bible. God, however, looked beyond their failures because each of these people was a man and woman of faith who took responsibility for their mistakes and failures. We have to learn that handling failure right, it will give us a start of a new opportunity.

We must know that destiny requires faith, faith requires taking risks, and risks come with failure. Something could go wrong. We have to prepare for it, for we cannot fulfill our destiny if we don't take any risks. Many people think they are unacceptable because they have failed. But grace abounds with failure according to the Scripture, and we can always handle it. What matters is what we do with failures.

For instance, we can either help people overcome a failure mentality, or we can keep them in their failure by accusations. We can either connect with them with Jesus Christ by lifting them, or we can accuse them like Satan. And let us never forget that grace empowers us to get out of failures. So step up and accept your failures. Come with a message of hope and faith for people groping in their failures so that positive change can happen in their lives.

KEYS TO DEALING WITH FAILURE

We see that great men and women of old did make mistakes, and a great number of them came out of it. So let us examine some of their lives and experiences so we can know and learn how they did, particularly David, the King of Israel as recorded 1 Chronicles 13:1-14. We mentioned in the previous chapter the Ark of the Covenant and the mistake Uzzah made.

First and foremost, we see that David's failure was a public spectacle; it was seen by the whole nation. It wasn't something that could be hidden. It was a national disaster. The whole nation saw and heard of Uzzah's death, resulting from David's mistake.

There were also several other mistakes that David made that caused the death of thousands. God did not destroy him but showed him where he went wrong. David acknowledged his mistakes and learned from his failures.

But how did David respond to his failure? The Scripture says, *"David was angry because the LORD had broken out against Uzzah."* 1 Chronicles 13:11 (ESV) Who do you think David was angry with? God of course! But David did something beautiful that we should imitate. He learned from his failure.

> *"Then David summoned the priests Zadok and Abiathar, and the Levites Uriel, Asaiah, Joel, Shemaiah, Eliel, and Amminadab, and said to them, "You are the heads of the fathers' houses of the Levites. Consecrate yourselves, you and your brothers, so that you may bring up the*

ark of the LORD, the God of Israel, to the place that I have prepared for it. Because you did not carry it the first time, the LORD our God broke out against us, because we did not seek him according to the rule." 1 Chronicles 15:11-13 (ESV)

Isn't that beautiful?

You see, David did not allow his failures to hold him back from his dream. Rather, he learned from his failures and became successful by doing things the proper way. This is what God desire of us in dealing with our mistakes. All failures and mistakes can be stepping stones to growth if we respond the right way.

OWN YOUR FAILURES

If you are struggling with what to do with your mistakes, the first thing to do, according to the Scriptures, is to own your failures. The Scripture says: *"Whoever conceals his transgressions will not prosper, but he who confesses and forsakes them will obtain mercy"* Proverbs 28:13 (ESV). That means that whosoever puts his arms around his mistakes, takes them home and becomes responsible for them, will prosper. That is how God wants us to deal with our mistakes. We are to put our arms around it, take it home and become responsible for it.

Conversely, if we cover our failures and mistakes, we cannot progress or move forward. So call your mistakes what it is: "I failed" or "I made a mistake" or, "I was wrong" or "I messed up." Own it, then change, and you will move forward.

Unfortunately, pride causes us not to own up but rather start to play the blame game like Adam, and King Saul did. Adam blamed Eve and God, while King Saul blamed people, circumstances, and God Because he just wanted to look good and be justified before all. That is pride.

But in all that, we still saw people who through humility admitted and acknowledged their wrongs. God came to their rescue, and they changed for the better.

In 2 Samuel 12:13, we see King David acknowledging His sins before the prophet Nathan in these words: *"I have sinned against the Lord."* He humbly admitted his wrong before the Lord. Humility is seeing life and things from God's perspective or point of view.

So let us not hide from failures but rather let us embrace them and learn from them. In so doing this, we must put away all forms of perfectionism and image-consciousness. While perfectionism is birthed out of failure and pride and is intolerant of people making mistakes, image-consciousness is wanting to look good at all costs as is the case of King Saul. Both of these are pride.

Remember, people who own their mistakes are much easier people to relate to.

Evaluate your Failures

To evaluate is to determine the significance, worth, or condition of something or a situation usually by careful appraisal and study. It means to form an opinion of the amount, value or quality of something after thinking about it carefully. That is what the Scripture in Proverbs 2:1-2 means when it says *"My son, if you receive my words and treasure up my commandments with you, making your ear attentive to wisdom and inclining your heart to understanding."* That is evaluation.

It is said that doing the same thing over and over again and expecting a different result is the definition of insanity. So the wise take their time to evaluate their mistakes, make corrections, learn from them and move on.

Whenever you see that you have made a mistake, do you have the feelings of disappointments or discouragement? Do you have the feelings of hopelessness? Or do your mistakes cause you shame and guilt? Does it make you ashamed or disheartened or inferior? You have got to find out what is going on in your heart at the instance of failure. That way you will be able to evaluate your mistakes accurately.

Responding to Failure

How do you respond when you fail? Do you play the blame game or admit your wrong? What pattern do you follow?

Adam covered his mistakes and blamed Eve and God and faced the consequences. Uzziah, the king, became enraged because the priest stopped him from burning incense before the Lord. His anger caused him to break out with leprosy.

Elijah, the prophet of fire, got depressed and withdrew when he was faced with a death threat from Jezebel. The great man of God, Moses, ran when the news of his act of murder spread. Instead of facing his mistake, he withdrew and ran.

The Apostle Peter wept when he realized his inconsistent nature resulted in his denial of Jesus. He went back to his old profession as a fisherman, going back to what he knew instead of standing up and carrying on doing all that Jesus had taught him.

So what do you do when you make mistakes? Get angry with yourself as some of the Bible characters we examined did? Blame yourself or others like they did? Give up or get distracted like they did? Deny and make excuses like some of them? Avoid it or try to compensate by pointing out an area of strength?

We know that it is hard for us to own up to our mistakes, but it is not supposed to be so. We are expected to be growing and taking on new challenges in faith, and that includes owning up to our mistakes and learning from them and making the necessary changes.

Don't forget this: God can take or use a mistake or failure to turn you around to get to your destiny and purpose.

Learn from your Failures

I think the greatest mistake anyone can make is not learning from his or her mistake. By not learning from your mistakes is a mistake in itself and to learn from your mistakes and move on might be the greatest knowledge you can gain in life.

According to the Scripture, we are to to use our failures to learn and gain wisdom. Proverbs 24; 30-32 has this say about learning from our mistakes: *"I passed by the field of a sluggard, by the vineyard of a man lacking sense, and behold, it was all overgrown with thorns; the ground was covered with nettles, and its stone wall was broken down. Then I saw and considered it; I looked and received instruction."*

The wise King of Israel said, in the concluding part of that Scripture, that he considered the situation well, looked upon it and then received instruction. We are to do like this king did - consider our failures well, look upon them and receive instruction or learning from them.

Now here are some questions you can ask to improve or prevent failure:

1. What did I do wrong? Always ask yourself this question when you make a mistake. The answer will start you on the road to restoration.

2. What did I do right? Was there anything you did right although you made a mistake? It is important you know this too.

3. What have I missed? Did you miss anything in the process of doing this thing that eventually resulted in a mistake?

4. What choices did I have? Did you have other alternatives that you should have considered and pursued instead of this one?

5. What are my weaknesses? What was your weakness in this situation? Could you have said that it was a weakness that caused it?

6. What can I learn? Now that the deed has been done, what can you then learn from this mistake?

7. What new skills did I learn? Can you point to any new skill that you learned from this mistake so you can use it to better my choices in your next move?

8. What support do I now have? What support, moral, mental and spiritual support, would you say you have received from people or some other sources?

The appropriate answers to these questions will put us a great deal down the road to learning from our mistakes.

Receive Forgiveness

Some people make mistakes and fail and then stay there instead of receiving God's forgiveness. They must receive forgiveness for themselves and then move on.

Forgiveness is very key in our walk with and in dealing with mistakes because it offers us a new and fresh start. Otherwise, we would never go forward again from where we fell. You can always trust the devil to do his job, for when we fail he will accuse us to the Father and to ourselves to erode and undermine our confidence. He does this because he knows that whatever is condemned or judged gets worse.

When we listen to Satan's accusations and condemnation instead of receiving forgiveness and moving on, we will get worse and withdraw from the field of play. But the truth of the Word of God makes it clear that forgiveness and grace release one to start again.

To receive forgiveness, we must, with all honesty, ask for it from God. When we must ask people to forgive us, we must not be too prideful, open up, talk to them and then apologize. In both cases, with God and with people, we do not need to accuse them but to simply seek forgiveness. We must understand that it is not enough or even good enough to say sorry to God. Rather, we should go a step further and talk to Him about the problem.

Take the time to tell God about it and let Him know how grieved you are about breaking the relationship. Then ask God further to forgive you for grieving the Holy Spirit because you know the Holy Spirit is involved in the relationship that was damaged. For the Holy Spirit, you should say, "Father, forgive me for grieving the Holy Spirit."

It is also important for us to know that even when our mistake affects people, e.g. causes damage to people, saying "I am sorry" is not also always enough. We must acknowledge how the relationship with them was damaged. Remember, a good meaningful apology acknowledges and understands how a person was hurt.

MOVE ON

We have evaluated our failures; we have learned from our failures, we have received forgiveness, now it is time to move on. The worst thing to do after our failures is to pack our bags, sit down and never try again. But now, we are going to move on. One of my favorite quotes from one of my mentors, Rick Loy, is "Never, never, never, never quit."

All great accomplishments require persistence. We saw that Moses kept on confronting Pharaoh until he got a breakthrough. That is the spirit of a champion. The Scripture is dotted with examples of men and women of faith, Moses, Elijah, Samson, Peter and more, who although they failed at one time or the other, dusted themselves off, picked themselves up and tried again.

LET IT GO

In your mistake, something died, so grieve over it and let it go. Sometimes you have to admit that something has ended, grieve over it once and for all, and let it go. It might be a relationship that we must let go of once and for all, never look back and never visit it again.

This is what the Scripture in Genesis 19:26 teaches us through the life of Lot's wife. She kept looking back instead of moving forward, and she turned into a pillar of salt.

In the final analysis, failure or loss should be grieved over like a dead person. We must then move on, knowing full well that God can bring good out of all things Romans 8:28. We can trust God to take the first step leading us to a fresh start. Don't forget: It is better to learn from little failures by dealing with them, so that by the time we need to deal with big failures we know what to do.

Do not throw away your confidence; it will be richly rewarded. You need to persevere so that when you have done the will of God, you will receive what He promised.

CHAPTER FIFTEEN - STRONGER

As we continue to grow into our rightful heirship as Kings in God's kingdom, we acknowledge that we do have weaknesses and make mistakes. What we do with our mistakes is what matters. We also know that we need to stay positive, admit our mistake, and receive forgiveness from God and then move on.

But for any King to be able to react positively to mistakes, he or she must be strong. It takes physical, mental, emotional and spiritual strength to keep going. But the best of all is spiritual strength, the source of all strength.

DIVINE DESIGN

First, we have to find out how man is constructed. In Genesis chapter 2 verse 7, the Scripture gives us an introduction to the design of man. Let us take a look: *"And the Lord God formed man of the dust of the ground, and breathed into his nostrils the breath of life; and the man became a living soul"* (KJV). This means that man is made in the image of God. We are a spirit being with a soul, dwelling in a body. That is you; that's your design.

Design Facts

Your spirit does not function according to the natural laws which govern this world. It is not subject or governed by the law of gravity or motion.

Your spirit is not limited in shape or size. That means even if a person is physically crippled or disabled, his spirit is not.

Your spirit provides energy and life force to your body and soul. The engine that drives the body is your spirit. When it is gone from the body; the body dies and becomes useless and helpless.

Spiritual authority flows out from within your spirit. This is a fact that is worthy of note: all spiritual authority is resident in the human spirit, and it is released from there.

> *"Keep your heart with all vigilance, for from it flow the springs of life."* Proverbs 4:23 (ESV)

Your spirit sustains your life

The Scripture puts it this way; *"As the body without the spirit is dead, so faith without deeds is dead."* James 2:26 (NIV). So what does this Scripture mean?

It means that your spirit provides energy and life to your soul and body. It is the driver of the soul and the body. If the spirit of a person is withdrawn, that person dies. That's clearly implied in the Scriptural verse above.

The human spirit can be broken, wounded, or crushed. I have never seen anything break a human spirit like careless words or actions. A broken spirit results mainly from unfair and inhuman treatments, experiences and disappointments. When a person's spirit is broken or wounded, he or she has less resistance to diseases, satanic attacks and all kinds of evil.

Your Spirit Energizes and Inspires Your Thoughts

Let's look at a second function of the spirit man: your spirit energizes and inspires your thoughts. The Scripture says it this way in Proverbs 20:27, *"As the body without the spirit is dead, so faith without deeds is dead."* In 1 Corinthians 2:11, it says, *"For who knows a person's thoughts except the spirit of that person, which is in him? So also no one comprehends the thoughts of God except the Spirit of God."*

We can conclude from those two scriptures that your spirit provides life and energy that flows from it. When your spirit flows, you can think clearly. As you speak and your spirit flows forth, your mind is 'quickened' with thoughts. Your spirit is like a flashlight, lighting up your soul and revealing your thoughts. The life of your spirit can manifest on your face. When people are full of life, there is a spiritual brightness or 'glow' on their face.

Your Spirit Flows out to Impact People

Let's look at yet another function of the spirit man: your spirit flows out to impact people. That impact is a function of the spirit, and real change occurs in people when you speak to them from your spirit man. This is how the Scripture puts it: *"Keep your heart with all vigilance, for from it flow the springs of life"* Proverbs 4:23 (ESV). Further, John 7:38 (NIV) says, *"Whoever believes in me, as the Scripture has said, streams of living water will flow from within him."*

Simply put, the influence of your spirit can 'flow' out beyond your body and impact the world around you particularly by the way you speak. In other words, through speaking, a person's spirit is released to flow out and impact people.

Have you ever been able to "feel" someone else's anger, or peace, or arrogance, or authority? Your spirit can be influenced by other people's spirit. You sometimes know, without looking, when someone sneaked up behind you. Or when someone is staring at you. Thus, it is important to make sure you are surrounding yourself with people who have a life-giving spirit.

Your Spirit Can be Strengthened

The Scripture says in Ephesians 3:16 (ESV) *"that He would grant you, according to the riches of His glory, to be strengthened with might through His Spirit in the inner man."* Unless Kings are strong inside, in their spirit, they can never be able to accomplish anything. They can never be strong to deal with life and mistakes.

The "inner man" refers to our spirit, which is joined to the Holy Spirit, who is the real man. The word "strengthened" in this scripture, according to Strong's Exhaustive Concordance of the New Testament means "to be empowered, made strong, and to increase in dominion and might[1]." The Strong's Concordance defines the word "might" as "supernatural ability, force, and militant ability[2]."

From those definitions, we can conclude that the source of the strengthening of our spirit is the Holy Spirit Himself. We are strengthened in our spirits by the Holy Spirit within us. The human spirit depends on the Spirit of God for the supply of its strength and might.

We need to learn how to cooperate with the Holy Spirit within us for strength and might. This is such an encouraging fact because we know that the spirit can be wounded and broken and, at such times, is helpless and hopeless, and may depend on another source for revitalization.

The revitalization or quickening we need comes from the Holy Spirit. We can count on Him because He is always stable and can never be wounded or broken like the spirit of man can be.

That being said, we must not forget that we have a role to play in this strengthening work of the Holy Spirit in our spirit. We as believers must take responsibility to develop and strengthen our spirit. Our part is to team up with the Holy Spirit particularly with speaking in tongues, meditating on and confessing the Word, and in walking in love for this strengthening to happen.

We see that our spirit can be strengthened. Even Jesus' spirit was strengthened: *"and the child grew and became strong in spirit, filled with wisdom. And the grace of God was upon Him"* Luke 2:40 (ESV).

So our spirit can be strengthened.

KEYS TO STRENGTHENING YOUR SPIRIT

If the spirit is that important, and it's strengthening that necessary for us to continue to be strong and making an impact in our world, then we need to find the keys to make this strengthening happen.

The Scripture says in 1 Corinthians 14:4 (ESV), *"The one who speaks in a tongue builds up himself,"* and in 1 Corinthians 14:14 (NIV), *"For if I pray in a tongue, my spirit prays, but my mind is unfruitful."*

By putting these two scriptures together, we can conclude that in praying in tongues, our spirit is exercised, strengthened, and built up. We give expression to words inspired by the Holy Spirit.

In praying or speaking in tongues, our spirit, soul, and body are energized with life. That's what the Scripture means by the word "edify," i.e., to build or construct a house.

It also helps to keep your mind focused on God.

Another key to strengthening the spirit is the practice of the regular confession of the Word of God. The Scripture says in John 6:63 (ESV), *"The words that I have spoken to you are spirit and life"* and in Hebrews 3:1 (ESV), *"consider Jesus, the apostle and high priest of our confession."*

The word "confession" in the above verse means "to speak the same thing, or to speak and embrace with confidence[3]." In other words, it means to speak or say the same thing as God. Spoken words release spiritual substance and spirit life.

God's words spoken from our spirit, and wholeheartedly embraced, impart spiritual strength and life. Confessing the Word of God activates the High Priest ministry of Jesus to open heaven's resources to us.

Confessing and holding on to the Word of God in the face of apparent failure, defeat and loss not only activates the high priestly ministry of Christ to us but also keeps Him on the job. The Word of God nourishes your spirit, so read it, write it, memorize it, pray it aloud, and meditate on it.

We also need to worship, which builds our intimacy with God. This takes the attention off of us and places it on the Lord Himself. In speaking in tongues and in confessing of the Word of God, we deal with ourselves, but in worship, we deal with God. Worship is the highest expression of the human spirit to God.

Here is what the Scripture has to say about this: *"And we all, with unveiled face, beholding the glory of the Lord, are being transformed into the same image from one degree of glory to another. For this comes from the Lord who is the Spirit"* 2 Corinthians 3:18 (ESV).

When we engage God in worship, there is a flow of life imparted from His Spirit to ours. In worship, the very life of God flows into us anew by the Holy Spirit. There is an impartation of His Glory, His nature, and goodness to us. In worship, the sweet gentle and generous nature of the Holy Spirit is imparted to us, working in us to manifest His fruits.

Strong praise enables our spirit to rise and encounter and experience the presence of God. In worship and in praise, the presence of the Lord is provoked, and that presence can become an experience to us. Our spirit easily engages the presence of God. But our souls and bodies need to be trained to allow our spirit to flow. We have to train our body to yield and to be expressive in worship. Focus your mind, will, and emotions by training your thoughts to stay fixed on Jesus until you feel your spirit arise and flow freely. In doing this, we are being transformed and metamorphosed inside and outside.

Exercising Your Spiritual Imagination

Spiritual imagination is a function of the spirit that makes for creativity and productivity. This process works in two ways: through meditation and through yielding to the Holy Spirit.

The Scripture says of this in 1 Timothy 4:15 (NKJV): *"Meditate on these things; give yourself entirely to them, that your progress might be evident to all."* The word "meditate" here means "to revolve in the mind, focus your interest upon, give repeated attention to, and constantly picture in your mind[4]."

Whatever you focus your attention on, you will open your heart up to. This is what is called the power of focus and attraction. Whatever we focus on grows. And whatever we focus on can be attracted to us. Repeated use of your spiritual imagination to picture and agree with the realities of God's Word opens your spirit to receive revelation and impartation.

The second aspect to exercising our spiritual imagination is through our yielding and obedience to the Holy Spirit of God. The Scripture says those *"who by reason of use have their senses exercised to discern both good and evil"*

Hebrews 5:14 (NKJV). Spiritual sensitivity and obedience to the Holy Spirit are developed by practice and accomplished through use.

Practice constantly by identifying spiritual impressions and sensations. That is why the scripture says through practice we exercise our senses to discern. This implies that we can make mistakes along the way, but as we keep on with the practice, we will bring ourselves to a level where we can tell what is good and what is bad without too much exertion. A blind man through the constant use of his other senses does not have a problem finding his way through a path or a room. That is what practicing will do for you.

So let us apply this to our lives by practicing speaking forth and exercising our God-given authority over our body, soul and circumstances. Practice speaking God's Word to your body, soul, circumstances and every other thing in your life and they will obey your voice.

Don't forget, each time you obey the Holy Spirit, your spirit becomes stronger. Each time you resist the devil, your spirit becomes stronger still.

"Finally, my brethren, be strong in the Lord and in the power of His might" Ephesians 6:10 (NKJV).

CHAPTER SIXTEEN - PRAYER

Prayer is the greatest and the most effective key to success in any endeavor so it must be one of the secrets to the success of Kings. Although we are beclouded by challenges, pain, pressure, and unexpected difficulties, through prayers as Kings, we can hold on and keep winning.

So as Kings, *"we do not look at things which are seen but at things which are not seen . . ."* 2 Corinthians 4:18 (NKJV). We must take our gaze and focus off the negative and challenging things that are happening around us. These things do not last because they are programmed by God to expire. Instead, we must set our gaze on the truth of the Word of God which is eternal. By doing this, Kings can hold in battle and come out victorious on the other side of the tunnel.

Even the challenges of life which the Scripture already concludes are temporary, can make or mar us, but each of us has to choose our response. Pressure and pain can lead to great personal growth if we respond the right way, knowing full well that those things are "working for us," to fashion, shape, and prepare us.

So the question is; what do you focus on? Pain or possibilities? Challenges, pressures and opportunities of the former time that are now over, or the new possibilities that God has waiting for you, tasks to accomplish, people to meet, relationships to establish and opportunities to serve?

The right thing to do is to focus on possibilities.

The Scripture calls you *"a chosen generation, a royal priesthood, a holy nation, His own special people that you may proclaim the praises of Him . . ."* 1 Peter 2:9 (NKJV). You are royalty, one with an assignment to serve as Kings through the power of prayer to focus on possibilities.

You are a King on assignment, so focus on your assignment which is to make Christ known to the world.

THE PRAYER OF KINGS

A few years ago I was introduced to a great book on prayer called the "Prayer of Jabez." The entire book was based on an account recorded in 1 Chronicles 4:9-10 (NKJV).

> *Jabez was more honorable than his brothers; and his mother called his name Jabez, saying, "Because I bore him in pain." Jabez called upon the God of Israel, saying, "Oh that you would bless me and enlarge my border, and that your hand might be with me, and that you would keep me from harm so that it might not bring me pain!" And God granted what he asked.*

According to the Scriptures, Jabez was a man of understanding. Jabez was a man with backgrounds and circumstances that were not his making. Although he was born without a choice as far these circumstances were concerned, he was able to come to the knowledge that these things ought not to be so. "These things are not normal and these conditions ought not to be so," Jabez quipped. "I cannot continue and be comfortable in these things and in this way of life," Jabez said. I believe the Spirit of God must have opened his mind to see the true nature of things because God wanted him to negotiate a change. No wonder the Scripture says that He was more honorable, more glorious, weightier and substantial than his brothers.

Jabez had a sense and a knowing that they did not have. He had a keenness of thought and a foresight that they never had. I believe he was a sober person, one who looks at things objectively and thoughtfully with deep questions and who, in turn, always sought change. He was a person who wanted to know. Such people are the ones that Scripture ascribes honor to. It is the glory of God to conceal things, but the glory of Kings is to search things out.

Have you ever seen a person called sorrow? I mean, of all the names in the world, the only one that Jabez's parents could think of was to name him sorrow. Well, that was the case of Jabez.

His mother named him sorrow because she bore him in pain. I do not fully understand the pain the mother was in when she gave birth to Jabez. Could it be that her husband, the father of Jabez, had died prematurely while Jabez was still in his mother's womb? This might likely be the case because nothing was said of the father naming him only the mother.

We know that in Jewish customs, the mothers don't name their children, but the fathers do. But in cases where the father is not available, either due to death, illness, the mother will have the transferred right to name the child or to confirm the name of the child as was the case of John the Baptist. In Luke 1:59-64 (ESV) tells us, *"And on the eighth day they came to circumcise the child. And they would have called him Zechariah after his father, but his mother answered, 'No; he shall be called John.' And they said to her,*

'None of your relatives is called by this name.' And they made signs to his father, inquiring what he wanted him to be called. And he asked for a writing tablet and wrote, 'His name is John.' And they all wondered. And immediately his mouth was opened and his tongue loosed, and he spoke, blessing God."

I believe this was the situation that Jabez mother found herself. Something must have happened to the husband in the course of her pregnancy that left her impaired with pain. She could not help than to name her child what she felt. The Scripture says, *"[God] calls into existence the things that do not exist"* Romans 4:17 (ESV). He does not call things the way they presently are but the way He intends them to be. This is a practice that we should adopt in every aspect of our walk with God which includes naming our children.

Well, for Jabez, the deed had been done. He grew up with that name and had come to be known by all with that name but what was he going to do? Live that name and the circumstances he found himself? Settle with that name as a norm? Accept the circumstances of his birth as normal and a comfort zone? Not Jabez! He had received an illumination from heaven. He broke out of his comfort zone. Jabez was set apart from his upbringing and his generation through prayer. This is why we know that prayer has the power to open the heavens and to change your future, and positively alter your destiny.

JABEZ PRAYER

As we see above, Jabez had more honor than His brothers although he had a circumstance of bitterness and sadness surrounding his birth. He was a person of glory and more weight and substance than his brothers.

We also see that Jabez stood out from circumstances and people because of his heart attitude. This is what makes successful kings

Jabez asked the Lord to enlarge his territory: *"Lord expand my influence and dominion."* This is the prayer of a King crying for God's favor and abundance!

We know that to enlarge means "to multiply and to increase in abundance[1]" as in Genesis 1:22. Kings desire to expand their territory and influence, i.e., to extend their Kingdom.

YOUR LIFE AND INFLUENCE

Jabez also spoke to God about his territory, asking God to enlarge it. Your territory as King is your life and influence. It is both invisible (your heart and inner life) and visible (your influence). Your territory is that which belongs to you, where your authority is recognized and where you have freedom to operate. It includes your skills, attitudes, family, emotions, relationships, hesitant fiancé, service, etc. It includes every area of your influence, both visible and invisible.

When you pray remember: *"Now unto him that is able to do exceeding abundantly above all that we ask or think"* Ephesians 3:20 (KJB). So what areas of your life are you determined to possess and to have as an enlarged territory? Your answer to that question will help to focus your mind on the characteristics of Jabez's prayer that we are about to discuss.

GETTING PERSONAL WITH GOD

Notice how many times the word "me" is used in the passage. It's about four times. Jabez got down to basics first and foremost by getting personal with God. We must understand that salvation is individual, and that relationship with God is individual. We must realize that God has a purpose and destiny for each of us individually. He has plans for good for us individually, and when we pray, we should approach Him for these individual plans.

He will answer us if we come in faith for the Scripture says: *"without faith it is impossible to please God"* Hebrews 11:6 (NIV). So make your prayer personal and do it in faith!

Also, we see that Jabez arose above his past pain and rejection and trusted the goodness of God. He did not allow rejection and sorrow, which were often roots of unbelief to detour him from having faith in God who answers prayers, to deter him. He knew that no matter what had happened to him, God was still good and still desired to bless and enlarge him. We should trust God the same way.

Whatever your heart issues, do not let unbelief hinder you from believing God and seeing His promises manifest in your life.

GETTING INTO THE PRESENCE OF GOD

Then we see Jabez making a request on the presence and person of God. He asked that God would bless him indeed, bless him in abundance. He asked God to shower favor and prosperity in abundance upon his life and relationships (v. 10).

In the New Testament, we discover we are redeemed so that the blessing of Abraham can come on us. So in redemption, we are blessed, and we should lay claim to it.

"Who has blessed us with every blessing in heavenly places" Ephesians 1:3 (ESV). We are blessed in Christ, and He has positioned us to walk in blessings. This is distinctive of the New Testament.

Now you might want to ask: How can we walk in and see the blessing that is already ours in redemption revealed and released upon us? First, we know that blessing is the overflow of intimacy with the Holy Spirit; He is the one who reveals what has been freely given to us by God. So what are we supposed to do?

We are to spend time in the presence of the Holy Spirit of God in worship. We are to spend time in meditation on the Word of God. We are to decree and declare His Word over our lives, relationships, and circumstances. This way we will have the blessing released and poured upon us.

GETTING THE PROVISION OF GOD

We are still focusing on the prayer of Jabez and particularly verse 10 where he asked God to enlarge his territory. A territory is a land to be possessed by driving out the occupants, giants, and dispossessing them of it. We know that there are always giants standing between us and God's provision. Giants are standing between you and the promised territory God has assigned to you.

In Exodus 23:30-31, God said to the children of Israel, through Moses, that He would drive out the inhabitants of the land and they would too: *". . . I will drive them out . . . you shall drive them out . . ."* This means that God and the children of Israel were going to do the driving out together. He would supply the strength and the courage, and the Israelites would supply their time, hands and swords.

In taking over our territories, God requires that we participate actively and not to be passive for we are in a partnership with Him. He promises to provide the thing that only God can provide and our part is to take faith actions by stepping out. God will supply the grace and ability through His Spirit in our spirit and we are to set goals, plan out our steps of actions, sow as necessary, persevere no matter what in the pursuit of taking the territories of the blessing of God and continue by His Spirit to overcome.

So what areas of your life and destiny do you desire an enlargement in this year, and what part must you play in co-operating with God?

Getting the Power of God

Still focusing on the prayer of Jabez, we look at another clause in his prayer that is worthy of note. In Verse 10, He prayed to the God of heaven again asking that His hand would be with him, *"oh... that your hand might be with me..."*

What is the hand of God, you might ask? The hand of God is the power of God manifested in a tangible way. It is God intervening and manifesting supernaturally in a way that you know it is He. We know that God desires to demonstrate His power, and to demonstrate His supernatural life. That is why the Scripture says that we should come to know through revelation something of the immeasurable greatness of His power toward us who believe.

But we know that the biggest and greatest hindrance to the flowing of the power of God is unbelief. You shouldn't be a person who is unbelieving but believing for all who believe are called to experience and manifest the supernatural life of God.

Power in the New Testament is connected with evangelism, which is a deliberate, conscious effort to make Christ known. If you want to see, experience and to walk in the power of God this year, you must be given to evangelism, and seek to make Christ known.

Getting the Protection of God

Jabez did not stop at asking God for enlargement, power, and provision. He also asked God for protection. He prayed saying: *"that you would keep me from harm"* (v. 10).

The days we live in are full of evil. Demonic opposition and temptation are a daily reality! The air about us is infested with evil spirits seeking to cause evil and destroy our usefulness with God. This is why Jesus said for us to *"Watch and pray that we may not enter into temptation"*

Matthew 26:40 (ESV). Jesus also prayed that God would deliver us from evil.

I have found one thing in life to be true and must admit it: we Kings can be vulnerable. Therefore, we must be truthful with ourselves and ask ourselves in what areas of our lives are we vulnerable. Is there a besetting of sin in our lives? When we come to terms with our vulnerability and figure out the areas of our vulnerability, we can find the strategy that we will cause us to overcome or to resist.

ARISE KING

It is your time and year of arising as Kings in faith, in prayer, and in action. Take some time right now and start praying consistently for an enlarging of your territory. Define the areas of your life you need or desire to enlarge. Ask yourself what must be done to make these changes. Take the steps necessary to prioritize and develop new skills that will aid you in accomplishing those changes with God's partnership. Look for new opportunities to serve, and take on new challenges. Recognize and respond to the Holy Spirit's promptings. You are enlarging your territory personally, locally, globally and globally this year!

Take your place!

PART FOUR
VICTORY

CHAPTER SEVENTEEN - VICTORY

Hell Week is a defining event of Navy Seal training. Hell Week consists of 5 1/2 days of cold, wet, brutally difficult operational training on fewer than four hours of sleep. Hell Week tests physical endurance, mental toughness, pain and cold tolerance, teamwork, attitude, and the ability to perform work under high physical and mental stress, and sleep deprivation. Above all, it tests determination and desire.

On average, only 25% of SEAL candidates make it through Hell Week, the toughest training in the U.S. Military. It is often the greatest achievement of their lives, and with it comes the realization that they can do twenty times more than they ever thought possible. It is a defining moment that they reach back to when in combat. They know that they will never, ever quit or let a teammate down.

Over the years, research has been done to determine a common trait in those individuals who make it through Hell Week. What the researchers found is that it's not necessarily the largest or strongest men, nor the fastest swimmers, who survive but those with burning desire to be SEALs. The only one true predictor of which candidates will ultimately succeed is those who want it the most[1].

We have come this far in life. We know the enemy and his tactics. We've learned from our mistakes. We've begun to step into the position given to us by Christ. We know the place and power of prayer in winning our battles. All of these things will do us no good if we are not ready to launch out into battle and fight. Now, it's our time to take our rightful place at the right hand of God and fight. It's time to get serious and want the victory.

Maybe you don't know your mandate and commission. Maybe you have not fully grasped what Jesus has commanded you to do at this time. In every culture and tribe, the words of a dying man are very important. But for you, the most important words are those of a Man, who was confirmed dead but came back to life. Jesus said to them again, *"Peace be with you. As the Father has sent me, even so I am sending you."* John 20:21 (ESV).

Maybe you do not think Jesus was referring to you and me. Or are you one who supposes that command was for only "the twelve"? So that you know, the apostle Paul was not among the twelve. Stephen and Philip were never among the twelve either, but they took the words of the Master seriously and personally because they were Jesus' followers as much as the twelve.

Jesus stated this: *"And what I say to you, I say to all"* Mark 13:37 (ESV).

GO WITH POWER

"After this the Lord appointed seventy-two others and sent them on ahead of him, two by two, into every town and place where he himself was about to go." Luke 10:1 (ESV)

We see in this Scripture that Jesus commissioned seventy-two disciples, in addition to the twelve apostles that he sent out before. This Scripture shows that Jesus' calling and sending process is unending, continuous and increasing. Jesus didn't give power and authority to just the first twelve apostles.

The word "appointed" here means "to lift something up to a new level, so as to disclose something that had previously been hidden[2]." The word "sent" is the Greek word *apostello* which means "to send forth on a mission[3]." It is from that word "sent" that we have the term missionary today. Thus, these believers received an apostolic commission to enter new places they had never been before to prepare people to encounter Jesus.

Unfortunately, many in the church have created a theology around the term Apostle, and have determined that only the apostles named in the New Testament received the power and authority, and such practice is not available to us today. That is a lie from the enemy to keep us at bay!

The word "apostle" means "a delegate, an ambassador, one who has been sent on a military mission as a representative of a kingdom[4]", literally "a sent one." From that word "apostle" comes another word "apostolic", the keyword that conveys what we are to be accomplishing in God's kingdom.

The word "apostolic" means to be sent forth from a New Testament local church and anointed with supernatural power. Now let me add that a believer may not necessarily be an apostle, but he or she can be sent and equipped with supernatural power just as an apostle. The picture Jesus had in mind was not to have a few selected people sent with the title "apostle." To Him, all believers are to be *apostello* meaning all believers are set free, set apart and sent out on a mission to the community with authority and power. No wonder Satan will try to convince the church not to receive this commission!

The word "mandate" according to the Webster's Dictionary means "a command or authorization to act[5]." It is an assignment entrusted to one by a higher authority. It also means an authorization to act as a representative or ambassador.

Ultimately, Jesus gave an "apostolic mandate" to all believers to go into the entire world to proclaim the Gospel and make disciples and do this with signs, wonders, and miracles.

THE FIRST APOSTOLIC MANDATE

"And God blessed them. And God said to them, "Be fruitful and multiply and fill the earth and subdue it and have dominion over the fish of the sea and over the birds of the heavens and over every living thing that moves on the earth." Genesis 1:28 (ESV)

It is important we know that mandates, as far as God is concerned, are not a new thing. It didn't just start with Jesus directing His disciples. At the very dawn of creation, God gave a mandate to our first parents, Adam and Eve. This mandate was a joint one, given to both the man and the woman, male and female. It was apostolic and was for both Adam and Eve, as it is for the twelve, then the seventy-two, and then to every believer today.

We can only understand our mandate by taking a critical look at the key words that make up the mandate.

First, God said to Adam and Eve, "Be fruitful" and to be fruitful means to bear fruit, to grow, to increase, and to be productive. I hope that suggests something to you. You and I are commanded and authorized by God to grow, to be productive and to be fruitful. We cannot be otherwise. I am authorized to bear fruits of souls and lives. What about you?

Secondly, God said in the mandate for them to "multiply" meaning to become numerous, reproduce. I wonder how many of you can say you have reproduced yourself in the last five years. Have you grow from just one Christian to a group of Christians? Reproduction is an authorization from heaven for us.

Thirdly, God said for them to "fill the earth" meaning they should cause the earth to flourish and to fulfill the purpose for which it was created by God. Adam and Eve were authorized by God to make the earth yield an increase, and to fulfill its created purpose. What a mandate! Adam and Eve had the power and authority to make the earth yield plentifully.

Fourthly, God said to them to "subdue the earth," to rule and reign over the earth as ambassadors of heaven as one with delegated authority. So conclusively, we can see that Adam and Eve were jointly commissioned, and sent by God into the earth to exercise spiritual authority and power, and to govern it as His representatives. This was the first and original mandate. All other mandates including the "Apostolic Mandate" of Christ stem from it.

Jesus' Apostolic Commission

"Jesus went through all the towns and villages, teaching in their synagogues, preaching the good news of the kingdom and healing every disease and sickness. When he saw the crowds, he had compassion on them, because they were harassed and helpless, like sheep without a shepherd. Then he said to his disciples, "The harvest is plentiful but the workers are few. Ask the Lord of the harvest, therefore, to send out workers into his harvest field." He called his twelve disciples to him and gave them authority to drive out evil spirits and to heal every disease and sickness." Matthew 9:35-10:1 (NIV)

It does no good to tell someone to do something that you have never done. The best form of leadership is leadership by example. Jesus had to show the disciples how to do things by doing it Himself. Afterward, He sent them to go in His authority to perpetuate what they saw Him do. Jesus did much to demonstrate His authority by healing sickness and disease before He sent them out to do the same.

It is important we know that Adam and Eve could but did not utilized the mandate God gave them because of sin. When they disobeyed God, they lost the authority and mandate they had received from God. Through their disobedience to God, Satan usurped their authority and today what was meant for the good of humanity. Satan now uses against the same humans who received the mandate initially.

Satan was so particular, sure and steadfast on this point that he made a bold declaration of his usurped authority to Jesus when he tempted Him. He tried to negotiate that authority for Jesus' worship, *"and said to him, 'To you I will give all this authority and their glory, for it has been delivered to me, and I give it to whom I will'"* Luke 4:6 (ESV).

Thank God for Jesus Christ! He never yielded to the devil for one second and in our redemption by His death, burial and resurrection, He set into motion the restoration of man and woman to a relationship with God that assures the original mandate and much more in Christ, if the person believes. Now everyone who believes in the atoning sacrifice of Jesus on the cross is restored back to God and empowered to fulfill God's purpose.

When Jesus was finished with the part of redemption that was for Him alone to do, He passed on the mandate God gave Him down to the disciples, but He did not stop there. He also did something more. He sent them the Holy Spirit to empower them to execute this kingdom mandate effectively. In that way, they became laborers with power and proofs.

> *"Then he said to his disciples, 'The harvest is plentiful, but the laborers are few; therefore pray earnestly to the Lord of the harvest to send*

out laborers into his harvest.' ... He called his twelve disciples to him and gave them authority to drive out evil spirits and to heal every disease and sickness. ... As you go, preach this message: 'The kingdom of heaven is near.' Heal the sick, raise the dead, cleanse those who have leprosy, drive out demons. Freely you have received, freely give." Matthew 9:37-38 and 10:1, 7-8 (NIV)

The word "authority" is derived from the Greek word *exousia* meaning "authority to speak and act on one's behalf[6]", in this case, Jesus' behalf. Today as it was 2000 years ago when Jesus gave the mandate to His early followers, He is still looking for men and women who will arise, take Him seriously, take Him at His word and go forth and exercise this dominion on His behalf.

YOU ARE DESIGNED FOR DOMINION

"For You have made him a little lower than the angels, And You have crowned him with glory and honor. You have made him to have dominion over the works of Your hands; You have put all things under his feet," Psalm 8:5-6 (NKJV)

Now you might be wondering where we are going with all this. Why all this talk and story about authorization to act for one mandate? It is so you and I will come to our place in Christ and take on the purpose of God with all boldness and confidence as an army, fully advancing and prosecuting a mission. It is for you that Jesus did all that He did. It is for you that He sent His Spirit to continue with the mandate through you.

In the original Hebrew language, the word translated as *"angels"* from Psalms 8:5-6 is the word *"Elohim"* who is God. God rules over angels and creation. We see that God designed man and gave him a place and position equal and next to Jesus. He also designed man to be His under-ruler over all creation and over all angels which originally included angel Lucifer or Satan.

The word *"crown"* in Psalms 8:5 refers to the ornamental headgear worn by a sovereign head of state which symbolizes his right to rule. You might be wondering and saying in your heart: how does that affect me? What do I have to do with sovereignty and with royalty?

According to the Scripture, you were born again by the Holy Spirit into the Family of God and that family is a royal one:

> *"But you are a chosen generation, a royal priesthood, a holy nation, His own special people, that you may proclaim the praises of Him who called you out of darkness into His marvelous light."* 1 Peter 2:9 (NKJV)

Royalty runs in your veins; you were born that way. By that birth, you are designed by God to exercise dominion on His behalf. By that birth, you are designed by God to subdue every satanic opposition to His rule and purpose.

The Scripture encapsulates your royal status and your exercise of royalty in these words.

> *"Let the saints be joyful in glory; Let them sing aloud on their beds. Let the high praises of God be in their mouth, And a two-edged sword in their hand, To execute vengeance on the nations, And punishments on the peoples; To bind their kings with chains, And their nobles with fetters of iron; To execute on them the written judgment -- This honor have all His saints."* Psalm 149:5-9 (NKJV)

The words *"kings"* and *"nobles"* in that Scripture are evil spiritual powers that oppress, and dominate people. But our calling from the Scripture is to confront and subdue these malevolent powers. God has designed that subduing these forces is an honor and privilege that God gives to all His people. God is pleased when He sees humans, flesh, and blood, seemingly weak creature compared to what went into the making of angels and other creatures of God, exercising dominion over spirit forces and powers that are supposed to be stronger than them. This is the wisdom of God that angels have not been able to understand.

God is pleased when He sees man ruling creatures like He would and does so just by issuing commands through the Word of His mouth. This makes man resembling God indeed. Of course, we know that the underlying weapon of this warfare is "words," words spoken and declared by God's authorized representative, you. God's Word declared through our mouths is the way we take dominion and rule for God in this realm of life. Don't forget this: to take dominion is to rule where God has assigned you, and release His Kingdom in the earth. More so, as we said in an earlier chapter, we should find out where God has placed us and then function from there if we are to be effective and win in spiritual battles.

You Have been Commissioned

"And Jesus came and spoke to them, saying, 'All authority has been given to Me in heaven and on earth. Go therefore and make disciples of all the nations, baptizing them in the name of the Father and of the Son and of the Holy Spirit, teaching them to observe all things that I have commanded you; and lo, I am with you always, even to the end of the age.' Amen." Matthew 28:18-20 (NIV)

From the preceding verse, we see that Jesus declared that He is the One with all the authority in Heaven and on earth and He turned all this authority over to the church to exercise for Him. By that statement alone, Jesus gave the church a commission and a command, not a suggestion to carry out for Him on His behalf.

This command or mandate, known by the church today as the "Great Commission," is primarily to make disciples or to disciple all nations. All nations include but is not limited to people, government, business, media, sport, arts, science, education, families; all levels of human existence and function. It is a mandate to influence and to change the culture of all nations. I hope that speaks volumes to you.

The world culture presupposes a people with the same language, values, geographical location and ancestral relation and inheritances. You and I know that to be able to influence we have to go to the nations; they are not coming to us. We cannot influence and change culture from within the church for this does not take place in church buildings! This can only take place when believers identify the territory God has entrusted to them in the world and then set about advancing the Kingdom of God in it. We are in the world to influence and change it with heaven's culture, and not the other way round.

Hence, we must understand spiritual authority, embrace it and then go ahead and exercise it. Go for it! Take your place!

CHAPTER EIGHTEEN - ARISE

Everything that God does with and in man always begins with a dream. Success begins with a dream. Triumph and victory begin with a dream, an inspiration, a stirring of the Holy Spirit in your heart for victory. This is because, in the kingdom, all we become is all we first see. We can become anything, but unless we first see it, we won't achieve it. We can win any battle in the kingdom, but unless we first see the victory, we won't achieve the victory. This is a principle of the Word of God.

We see God, in dealing with Abraham, say to him: *"as far as your eyes can see."* This is because everything begins with seeing first *"The LORD said to Abram, after Lot had separated from him, 'Lift up your eyes and look from the place where you are, northward and southward and eastward and westward, for all the land that you see I will give to you and to your offspring forever.'"* Genesis 13:14-15 (ESV).

Years after God told Abraham to see by faith into the inheritance He had given him, He came in a more vivid form to one of Abraham's great-grandsons, Joseph. God does not change so He came again to Joseph first by giving dreams, because until one sees, he cannot become.

The Scripture declares in Genesis 37:1-10 that Joseph dreamed a dream. Dreams and visions are the language of the Holy Spirit. They are pictures of the future and possibilities, and through them, God reveals His plans and purposes to us.

> *"Jacob lived in the land of his father's sojournings, in the land of Canaan. These are the generations of Jacob. Joseph, being seventeen years old, was pasturing the flock with his brothers. He was a boy with the sons of Bilhah and Zilpah, his father's wives. And Joseph brought a bad report of them to their father. Now Israel loved Joseph more than any other of his sons, because he was the son of his old age. And he made him a robe of many colors. But when his brothers saw that their father loved him more than all his brothers, they hated him and could not speak peacefully to him. Now Joseph had a dream, and when he told it to his brothers they hated him even more. He said to them, "Hear this dream that I have dreamed: Behold, we were binding sheaves in the field, and behold, my sheaf arose and stood upright. And behold, your sheaves gathered around it and bowed down to my sheaf." His brothers said to him, "Are you indeed to reign over us? Or are you indeed to rule over us?" So they hated him even more for his dreams and for his words. Then he dreamed another dream and told it to his brothers and said, "Behold, I have dreamed another dream. Behold, the sun, the moon, and eleven stars were bowing down to me." But when he told it to his father and to his brothers, his father rebuked him and said to him, "What is this dream that you have dreamed? Shall I and your mother and your brothers indeed come to bow ourselves to the ground before you?"* Genesis 37:1-10 (ESV)

You might say, "But that is Old Testament times. God does not do that now in this day in age." Here's what the Scripture says: *"In the last days, God says, I will pour out my Spirit on all people. Your sons and daughters will prophesy, your young men will see visions, your old men will dream dreams"* Act 2:17 (ESV). You see dreams are still for today. God, in that Scripture, gave us a divine bucket list. You can put your name and the name of your sons and daughters on it.

From the story of Joseph, it is clear to the believer of today that God has destined us to be fruitful. You and I are today's "Joseph" in every area of life in which we find ourselves. In the Scripture, it says of Joseph's mother: *"She conceived and bore a son and said, 'God has taken away my reproach.' And she called his name Joseph, saying, 'May the LORD add to me another son!'"* Genesis 30:23-24 (ESV). God has taken away your reproach, and He will add to you.

Your prophetic destiny is to add to, to be productive and to be fruitful. All believers are called to be part of this prophetic blessing of addition and fruitfulness. Jesus made this clear in the Scriptures when He said in John 15:16 (NIV) *"You did not choose me, but I chose you and appointed you so that you might go and bear fruit--fruit that will last--and so that whatever you ask in my name the Father will give you."* Jesus has chosen you to bear fruit. He does the choosing, and we do the bearing of fruits. He said, *"I chose you to bring forth fruit."* He chooses us.

It is clear, from the Scripture above, that fruit bearing is an overflow of a life that draws upon the Holy Spirit and the Word of God. It is the overflow of abiding in Christ, His life coming forth through the one who abides. We can never bear fruit apart from a living, thriving relationship with the Holy Spirit and the Word.

KINGS DREAM

As royalty, we begin our rule by dreaming, by seeing into the future, through visions, thoughts and revelations. I believe this is why the Scripture in Ephesians 3:20 says *"that God can do abundantly more than we ask or think."* God does the things that we see in our minds and hearts by the Spirit. Kings dream otherwise they are not kings. As kings, we must explore all the realms of possibilities. We are royalty, and we have an identity.

Every king dreams of extending his kingdom. As royalty, we must dream of extending the kingdom of God we represent. We have said before and would be worth reiterating here that dreams are supernatural influence and inspiration into our life as they were in Joseph's life. God communicates on a constant basis in dreams, visions, trances and inspired thoughts.

This was the way God communicated with the Patriarchs of the Faith: Abraham, Joseph, and Jabez. These men were inspired in life through dreams. You and I can also dream today. We can dream of dominion, and we can dream of significance. We can dream of a life of influence, and we can do all this by the Word of God.

You do not have to sleep and have a dream before you can conclude that God is speaking to you. The Word of God is the dream of God for us. The Word of God can come to you and form a dream of the future and influential life. Dream the Word, or dream by the Word of God. Let the Word of God form dreams in you. For this to happen, we must position ourselves. We must position ourselves by learning to be alone with God, by learning to focus on God and His Word alone, and by learning to be quiet and to give ourselves to meditation. Many of the dreams we celebrate today were born in the place of meditation and quietness.

KINGS DECLARE THEIR DREAMS

In the kingdom of God, it is dreams declared or proclaimed that become realities. Joseph knew about this, which is why he had to tell his dream to his brothers and to his father although they later hated him for it. It is only dreams that are declared that have the capacity of fulfillment. Until God's Word is gone forth out of our mouth, it is not clothed with the power of divine fulfillment (See Genesis 37:5, 9 and 10).

Although Joseph did not understand everything about his dream, yet he spoke and declared the Word of God - his dream. He set into motion the power of the Word of God so that it would not be void of fulfillment. He keyed into a principle that he didn't even know about. He exercised the power of the tongue when he spoke forth his dreams. He knew that our words, God Words spoken from our lips, shape our spiritual atmosphere and create room for the invisible to become visible.

Therefore, we must learn to use our tongue in speaking forth our dreams of the Word, thereby creating the spiritual atmosphere that makes for the fulfillment of the dream. You must know that declaring the Word of God over your life on a daily basis shapes and frames your future. By doing this, the events that will make for the fulfillment of your dream will be triggered. Take advantage of this ability.

KINGS PREPARE

The Scripture makes it clear that dreams and visions have an appointed time for their fulfillment. Dreams don't just fulfill themselves, but we have a role to play in their fulfillment. This is why the Scripture says, *"Faith without works is dead"* James 2:26 (ESV). In this sense, faith is the dream and works is our action on the dream.

We understand that dreams don't just come to pass just by dreaming but by actions which include speaking and having an ordered life, a life totally yielded to the Holy Spirit and the Word. The Scripture warns that meaningless dreams, dreams that have no foundation and can never find fulfillment, come through much activity (Ecclesiastes 5:3).

Dreams have a time period attached to them for their fulfillment. That means that there is a timing element for dreams to manifest and find fulfillment. In Psalm 105:19, the Scripture says of the time when Joseph's dream was fulfilled - when the king sent for him and loosed him from prison. His dream's time had come. *"Until the time that his word came: the word of the LORD tried him"* Psalm 105:19 (KJV).

We must learn that we must cooperate and play our part in the fulfillment of God dreams for our lives.

Joseph's Preparation

If dreams don't fulfill themselves, if we have a part to play in their fulfillment and if every dream has a time for its fulfillment, what are we supposed to do to prepare ourselves for the ultimate fulfillment during our waiting time? Let us see how and what Joseph did when his time had not yet come, and his dream was still hanging in the balance.

During Joseph's time of waiting, we discover he was serving, he was learning, he was digging, and he was growing in capacity to lead and accomplish things. First, he worked for Potiphar, then he served in the prison. During this the time, God placed Joseph in the place and position of leadership and administration through circumstances so he would be furnished thoroughly to handle his dream when its time of fulfillment finally came.

> *"And Joseph found grace in his sight, and he served him: and he made him overseer over his house, and all that he had he put into his hand. And it came to pass from the time that he had made him overseer in his house."* Genesis 39:4-5 (KJV)

> *"And Joseph's master took him and put him into the prison, the place where the king's prisoners were confined, and he was there in prison. But the LORD was with Joseph and showed him steadfast love and gave him favor in the sight of the keeper of the prison. And the keeper of the prison put Joseph in charge of all the prisoners who were in the prison. Whatever was done there, he was the one who did it."* Genesis 39:20-22 (ESV)

We see that God, through circumstances, placed Joseph in places that prepared him for his dream and during all of those times, he prospered in the things he did. No wonder Joseph also prospered or succeeded in administering Egypt and its resources when the time came for the fulfillment of his dream. In every circumstance, Joseph developed skill and capacity in different environments that eventually fitted him for his place of destiny and glory. He was not a novice in matters of administration and leadership. So how are you preparing yourself for the ultimate fulfillment of the dream God gave you?

It is said that a man of gifts and talents can climb to any position even in a twinkle of an eye, but it will take a man of character to keep that position. Talents, skill and learning are not enough for us to fulfill the dream of God has for our lives no matter how good they may be; we need character too.

It takes character for a person who was betrayed and sold into slavery to say later to his betrayers that it was God who sent him through their betrayal to be ahead of them to preserve them. That is a person who has developed the character of the Spirit strongly.

I do not know, except through the guide and understanding of the Spirit, how a person that was hated, betrayed and rejected, one who suffered injustices and planned temptation, could end up saying all of that was God sending him. And I do not know how a person could appeal to those same persons who hated and betrayed him so that he suffered these things in their hands and asked them not to be grieved. That's character!

> *And Joseph said to his brothers, "Please come near to me." So they came near. Then he said: "I am Joseph your brother, whom you sold into Egypt. But now, do not therefore be grieved or angry with yourselves because you sold me here; for God sent me before you to preserve life."* Genesis 45:4-5 (NKJV)

From the way Joseph conducted himself and talked to his brothers at the end of his life we see that he had developed in grace, wisdom and generosity. He had grown in strength and in faith.

> *Joseph said to them, "Do not be afraid, for am I in the place of God? But as for you, you meant evil against me; but God meant it for good, in order to bring it about as it is this day, to save many people alive. Now therefore, do not be afraid; I will provide for you and your little ones." And he comforted them and spoke kindly to them.* Genesis 50:19-21 (NKJV)

Did you see that?

Joseph said to his betrayers that he will provide for them and their little ones. There was no air of vengeance, unforgiveness, or pay-back in his attitude and voice. That's maturity; that's character.

> *Joseph is a fruitful bough, A fruitful bough by a well; His branches run over the wall. The archers have bitterly grieved him, Shot at him and hated him. But his bow remained in strength, And the arms of his hands were made strong by the hands of the Mighty God of Jacob (From there is the Shepherd, the Stone of Israel)* Genesis 49:22-24 (NKJV)

Joseph had become strong by the Word as he learned to rest in it, and trust in it totally and completely. In spite of the bitter words, hatred and injustices that were sent against him, in spite of the words spoken against him, the arrows shot at him through the words of others, Joseph held on to the Almighty and to his Word. The Almighty, in turn, made his arms strong and brought him into fruitfulness.

This was the story of Joseph. It is not only his story; it is the story of everyone who says 'yes' to the apostolic mandate given us by the Lord. We will have troubles in the course of executing the mandate. But if we hold onto the Word as Joseph did, we will come out at the top in victory like Joseph. Let us hold for the time that the Lord will come through for us for He *"made everything beautiful in its time"* Ecclesiastes 3:11 (ESV).

Identity Crisis

You and I know the greatest crisis in the world and in the church today is the identity crisis. People don't know who they are. Moreover, Christians don't know who they are, and what Jesus in His death, burial and resurrection gave them.

The greatest issue in the identity crisis among Christians is the issue of understanding redemption and righteousness. We do not know that we have been bought and paid for by the blood of Christ. We do not know that we have been completely ransomed and freed from the hold of the devil. We do not know that we are at peace with God, that we have become friends with Him by way of righteousness. God is not holding anything against us, and Satan has no right to hold anything against us.

We have become, by virtue of redemption and righteousness, the very children of God, begotten through His Word and His Spirit in righteousness and holiness of truth. We are, by redemption and righteousness, royalty, priests of the Most High God, chosen and called of God for a His own special service.

Peter, contemplating our privileged position in Christ with God, was inspired by the Holy Spirit to write: *"But you are a chosen people, a royal priesthood, a holy nation, a people belonging to God, that you may declare the praises of him who called you out of darkness into his wonderful light"* 1 Peter 2:9 (NIV).

The Holy Spirit says that you are a "You are a chosen generation, a royal priesthood." And that's it. So what are we supposed to do? Agree with what God says we our identity. See ourselves the way God sees us, believe in ourselves as God believes in us, accept by faith who He says we are, live it and walk in it.

That we are a "chosen generation" means that we are selected by God to carry His DNA and be his family. What an honor! We are not *trying* to carry His DNA; we have it already. That is why we are royalty. We know that royalty is by birth and not by any other way. "For you have been born again, not of perishable seed, but of imperishable, through the living and enduring word of God" 1 Peter 1:23 (NIV).

As if being a "chosen generation" was not enough, the Holy Spirit says that we are a "royal priesthood," which gives us direct access to the very throne of God. No matter how royal and majestic a king is, his two-year-old child doesn't think twice nor is afraid to climb up onto the throne and fall into the king's arm. That's the relationship we have and enjoy with our King of Kings. The Word of God does not just say we are priests. That in itself is good enough. But it adds that we are royal, kingly and regal as priests of God. We are a combination of the functions of a king and a priest together in one. What a privilege!

As kings, we don't beg, we don't think like a victim, we don't think and act powerless, and we do not live our lives blaming others. We are loaded and decked out with awesome privileges. We make decrees, legislate, issue commands and give orders. We rule with authority for we are deputized to act in the affairs of this world for the King of Kings

As kings, we find out what our great King wants to be done through us. We listen to His will and purpose, then we declare that will and purpose to advance the Kingdom. We must not forget that as under-regents, we are ruling in the stead of our Sovereign King in this place in life. We do it for the King who is our King because *"He is King of Kings and Lord of Lords"* Revelation 19:16 (NIV). Glory to God! We are the ones in charge on this side of life for the King of Kings. God is counting on you and on me to do this work.

It will be well for you to know that Jesus is raising generations of kings and lords to advance His Kingdom on the earth. His goal is to duplicate Himself in you and in me, such that the kingdom will have many kings and many priests. What a selfless King we have! We are the generation of kings and lords. Let us take our place.

KINGS RECEIVE PROPHETIC DIRECTION

As we consider specifically kings and how they receive direction to advance their kingdom, it would be well for us to take a clue from the King of Kings Himself in His earthly life and ministry. Turning to the Gospel in the book of Mark 4:35, we see Jesus talking to His disciples and giving them direction as to their next move and plan of action.

And the same day, when the evening was come, he saith unto them, Let us pass over unto the other side. Mark 4:35 (KJV)

It is amazing how much the Bible says about evenings. We know that it was in the cool of the day that God always come walking in the Garden of Eden to fellowship with Adam and Eve and give them instructions. It was in the evening that Isaac went to the field to meditate when his bride arrived. There is something about evenings as far as the Scripture is concerned.

Why are evenings so important for giving directions from the King to His kings? It is because "eve", or evening as other translations put it, is the beginning of a new day. We see this in the Genesis account of creation; that day began in the evening. *"And the evening and the morning were the first day"* Genesis 1:5 (KJV). Today, the Jews still count their day beginning with the evening. In other words, their day starts at 6:00 p.m. in the evenings.

Symbolically, "evening" begins a new day, and new day means new opportunities, new challenges, and new experiences. No wonder God gives direction in the evening. When your day is still fresh and new, isn't it the best time to receive fresh ideas and instructions as to how to go about the day? That is why we see God always in the business of doing new things, fresh things in the evening.

Kings don't live in yesterday's experiences. They look forward to experiences in a new day. *"Give us today, our daily bread,"* the King of Kings taught His under-kings to pray for every new day requires new direction and new revelation.

In the Bible, when the evening came, Jesus gave His disciples the Word. When we are rightly positioned and set for the Word of instruction from the King, He will speak, His word will come, and His voice will break forth to us. We have to position ourselves to hear daily from God in a place of meditation, prayer and in the study of the Word.

A word of caution: Kings don't live in and on past experiences, or yesterday's revelation and experience. They wait for new bread every day through the discipline of rising up to meet the Lord early in the morning like Jesus, Abraham and Moses usually did. It is a fact that God releases His Word with the dew. Alone with God, in the early hours of the day, the King will give direction and revelation to His kings. So cultivate the habit of being alone with God and of rising early in the morning for an everyday meeting with the King for instructions and for direction.

KINGS DREAM OF ENLARGING THEIR TERRITORY

Territories. How much territory is under a king's control and rule is proof of how powerful that king is. Earthly kings naturally want more territory. They even want to have kings of other lands paying tribute to them, bowing to them and serving them. I hope you know what it means for one king to bow down to another king in surrender. It is power and pride for the standing king and humiliation for the bowing king. Earthly kings take territories thereby seeking expansion of their kingdom.

Jesus, the King of Kings, would not do less.

> *On the same day, when evening had come, He said to them, "Let us cross over to the other side.* Mark 4:35 (NJKV)

Every king seeks to always cross over, to travel and journey to new places. This is what we are our King demands from us so we must be willing to move forward, to enlarge, and advance from our current positions to other new positions.

There will be challenges and obstacles to be faced in the expansion of territories, but that does not in any way detour the king's advancement. For a king that knows himself, that have the right strategies and resources, every opposition and challenge can be faced with confidence. Let us be prepared to journey to places of new opportunities, knowing that our King and God is with us.

We have established that taking territories are a king's delight. Now, Jesus understood this fact more than anyone of us. We know from the words of Christ that the "other side" in His Words means the territory beyond the place He and His disciples were standing. And in this case, it was the country of Gaderenes.

God, the King, wants us to take on new territory. He wants us to take on new areas. He wants us to invade and advance the kingdom into new lands and areas. He wants us to take on new areas in our personal life, new unoccupied territories in our finances, and new territories in our marriage and other people's marriages. God wants us to break new grounds and have new experiences in ministry, in finances, in family and much more.

Whichever way and in whatever area, God calls every generation out of their security to advance the kingdom in every level of life! God expects us to break into all sectors of the human society to advance His kingdom. He expects us to advance His kingdom in the media world, in the educational sector, in arts and culture, in government, in politics, in sciences.

I think it will be well for us to know and to ask ourselves what dream do we have of the future enlargement and advancement of the kingdom of God on the earth. Without you, God can't.

KINGS ADVANCE NEW TERRITORY

In taking territories, there is so much that kings must do to avoid distraction and stay focused on their course. The Scripture says of Jesus in the advancement of His territory of His earthly ministry that *"they left the multitude and took Him along on the boat"* Mark 4:36 (NJKV).

Kings aren't led by the crowd and multitudes. Kings don't flock around with every Tom, Dick and Harry. More often than not, the "crowd" usually lacks vision. They are the followers, the dream stealers. The ones who feel entitled to receive assistance, but are not willing to work to get it.

If you get too involved with the "crowd", they will pressure you to conform and what they like, do what everyone else is doing.

Kings are people of, and with, vision, direction, and courage. A distinctive character of kings is that they hear from God before they take any step. Because they hear from God, they are people with vision and new drive to take on new territories.

Kings walk by faith, and we know that the faith life is a journey of hearing from God and moving forward. It takes faith to strive and to advance God's kingdom. It takes courage to face an enemy upfront and fight to victory. It takes faith and courage to take on new frontiers and territories without getting side-tracked and kicked.

What can a person who doesn't take risk achieve with life? What will a king accomplish who likes to sit in his comfort zone of life and not take on new territories? Unless you take risks and move out of your comfort zone, you can never experience any great adventures. Cast off from shore!

There definitely will be uncertainties as you launch into unknown and unexplored lands, but there is no need to hold back. It is better to move into uncertain territories than to be stay stuck in familiar territories living in the glories of the past. No general is ever satisfied with battles. He knows after one battle is won, there is yet another to take on. And it is in the battles fought and won that his glory and stardom is revealed.

So what are you afraid of? What is holding you back? What are you clinging to? Step out in obedience and by faith take on territories for the Master. Yes, faith journeys seem lonely, but we are not alone. You are not alone. Jesus is with you. Moreover, you are not the only one in the journey. Other people are taking the same journey, moving and marching to advance the King's kingdom in new lands.

Go for it and let your faith be a motivation for others.

KINGS HAVE A SPIRITUAL PERSPECTIVE

"A great windstorm arose, and the waves were breaking into the boat." Mark 4:37 (ESV)

Let's look at another very important aspect in advancing Kingdom territory. We must know that in taking territories, many things are involved.

We see Jesus coming face to face with oppositions to His advances as well. In Mark 4:37 and 5:2, Jesus met opposition in the storm on the sea on His way to the new land and as he encountered a demonized man as soon as He stepped into the territory.

With this, we discover that every assignment God assigns will attract demonic opposition in people and in circumstances. There will be storms and turbulence on the way, and demons to confront in the land, but we are assured of one thing: *"But thanks be to God, who in Christ always leads us in triumphal procession, and through us spreads the fragrance of the knowledge of him everywhere."* 2 Corinthians 2:14 (ESV)

Jesus faced demonic oppositions in carrying out His task of advancing God's kingdom. We too we face them. But Jesus never lost His spiritual perspective.

It is worthy to see how the disciples responded to the opposition. They feared, complained, and became discouraged; they lost spiritual perspective. We see them consumed by the fear of death; we see them burying their faces and complaining and blaming. We see their faith was quenched for they were in doubt. They lost focus completely on the assignment and placed it on saving themselves. They started thinking like victims instead of kings. In the face of opposition, we have the tendency to behave like these early followers of Christ, but we also have every reason not to.

Does that look like you and me? Well, we don't have to react like this. Every time we give in to complaint and doubt in the face of opposition, we miss, by that act, the opportunity for growth.

KINGS MAKE DECREES AND ASSERT DOMINION

"Jesus woke up, he rebuked the wind and said to the waves" Mark 4:39 (ESV)

This is amazing! We have a lot to learn from the King of Kings Himself. The disciples were complaining and wailing about the storm because they had not properly come to grips with their identity in God. Jesus, the King, knew His identity. He looked at the storm and rebuked it.

Jesus knew that, as King, he could legislate, decree, give orders and command for He knew that *"where the word of a king is, there is power"* Ecclesiastes 8:4 (NJKV). He would not hesitate to issue a command that must be obeyed by whatever force. Jesus knew it was His territory and, because kings make decrees and assert their authority over their territory, He did not think twice before He gave the word of command: *"Peace, be still."* Mark 4:39 (ESV)

Do you arise in your spirit like a king for battle or do you cringe like a victim when oppositions come? And they will surely come. Wherefore, whatever your assignment or territory, you must learn to address the demons by faith and not doubt until you see them bow in fear and flee in terror. This is what God requires of us: faith, a life and walk of faith, and with no fear or doubt. Jesus, our King today, requires and expects us to interact with circumstances and opposition as kings and take dominion over them. We are not to do otherwise.

CHAPTER NINETEEN - AUTHORITY

In U.S. Navel Institute Proceedings, the magazine of the Naval Institute, Frank Koch illustrated the importance of obeying the Laws of the Lighthouse:

Two battleships assigned to the training squadron had been at sea on maneuvers in heavy weather for several days. A lookout was serving on the lead battleship and was on watch on the bridge as night fell. The visibility was poor with patchy fog, so the captain remained on the bridge keeping an eye on all activities.

Shortly after dark, the lookout on the wing reported, "Light, bearing on the starboard bow."

"Is it steady or moving astern?" the captain called out.

The lookout replied, "Steady, Captain," which meant they were on a dangerous collision course with another ship.

The captain then called to the signalman, "Signal that ship: 'We are on a collision course, advise you change course twenty degrees.'"

Back came the signal, "Advisable for you to change course twenty degrees."

The captain said, "Send: 'I'm a captain, change course twenty degrees.'"

"I'm a seaman second-class," came the reply. "You had better change course twenty degrees."

By that time the captain was furious. He spat out, "Send: 'I'm a battleship. Change course twenty degrees.'"

Back came the flashing light, "I'm a lighthouse."

The ship changed course.[1]

GOD OF ORDER AND AUTHORITY

Now I want you to realize that the head of every man is Christ, and the head of the woman is man, and the head of Christ is God. 1 Corinthians 11:3 (NIV)

All authority heads up in God. He is the God of order and authority. He set authority in place both in heaven and on earth. He determined that all things, angelic and human, find their expression by being connected to Christ, who in turn, is connected to Him, God the Father. In order of authority: God the Father is head and supreme, Jesus follows, then the family man and then the wife. This is why the Scripture says that Christ is the head of the man, the man is the head of the woman.

As head, the man/husband has the role of leadership to play to his wife and his family. He is placed in the place of leadership over his family to give direction and guidance. God designated him thus. In the matter of authority, God has placed greater authority on the man, although both he and the wife are of equal value.

Authority in the family is God's organized way of fulfilling His purposes on the earth through the family. As one in authority, the father is responsible for protecting those under his authority or of lesser authority.

This is the way God deals with us too. He gives authority and being the Supreme Authority. He protects us who are under His authority.

The Interaction of Spirit World/Human World

The Scriptures teaches that God is a God of order who created an orderly universe. No wonder someone once said, "order is heaven's first law." His kingdom works and runs on order. Order is heaven's first law.

God created an ordered universe.

> *What is man, that thou art mindful of him? and the son of man, that thou visitest him? For thou hast made him a little lower than the angels, and hast crowned him with glory and honor. Thou madest him to have dominion over the works of thy hands; thou hast put all things under his feet* Psalm 8:4-6 (KJV)

From Scripture, we can see the creative order of God. He created an orderly universe with rules and principles set over it, both for the unseen or spiritual, and the seen or natural worlds. God didn't leave anything to chance. We find out from the Word that one of the most important rules is the one that governs authority relationship. In other words, all created beings in the universe are ordered in the hierarchy of authority set in place by God. This authority relationship covers the angelic world, the human world and even the world of demons.

For the angelic world's hierarchy, we have angels in positions, of Archangels like the angels Michael and Gabriel and Lucifer, before his fall. After the Archangels, who are superior in ranks and authority, come the Cherubim, God's throne guardian angels. Next to the Cherubim are Seraphim, specially crafted for their mission of worship, and then are all the other angels.

Among the ranks of the demonic beings, first comes their leader, Satan, a corrupted archangel. Next, come the principalities, Satan's principal malevolent spirits. Following the principalities are the powers. These occupy a rank different from those of the principalities, as they are subject and obedient to the principalities. Then come the rulers and finally the demons. As you can see, everyone occupies a certain rank and place of authority in the kingdom of darkness. They know too well not to break their ranks.

Human beings, or mankind, are not left out in the place of authority and order as part of the creation of God. The place of human beings is so strategic and contentious. It was mankind's place that Satan coveted so much that he tried to trick him out of it through deception and falsehood, Satan knows so little about the universe around him that he cannot see that he only occupies the world until his lease is over on the earth. Man is, by design, created to rule over angels (1 Corinthians 6:3).

For man, authority and order extend from government to work to church and home; everyone in their place. There is a governmental authority that we must obey: *"Let every soul be subject to the governing authorities. For there is no authority except from God, and the authorities that exist are appointed by God. Therefore whoever resists the authority resists the ordinance of God, and those who resist will bring judgment on themselves"* Romans 13:1-2 (NKJV).

There are church governments that we must submit to and obey. God set them in place: *"Obey those who rule over you, and be submissive, for they watch out for your souls, as those who must give account. Let them do so with joy and not with grief, for that would be unprofitable for you"* Hebrews 13:17 (NKJV). And there is the authority at home, the husband, shared with the wife, that the children must obey and submit to. God never leaves us to chance. *"Children, obey your parents in the Lord, for this is right."* Ephesians 6:1 (NKJV).

As loving and wonderful as God is, even in the order of authority and rule, He still leaves us with a choice to either obey or disobey and never compels us. But He has set in motion consequences that naturally come on those who violate violators and resent these authorities and orders.

The first person in the created universe of God, who tried to break God's authority and order, was Satan, the devil. He thought he would not suffer any consequences, but he was wrong. Satan was required, as was every other of God's creations, to obey His rules strictly. However Satan, by choice, violated them and reaped the consequences thereof, confinement to working perpetually in darkness.

It is clear from Scripture that God created laws and principles that govern the natural and spiritual realms, and He upholds them by His power. And as it relates to this created authority, the laws, and principles, there are only two positions we can take towards what God has ordered, "submit" or "rebel."

> *"Everyone must submit himself to the governing authorities, for there is no authority except that which God has established. The authorities that exist have been established by God. Consequently, he who rebels against the authority is rebelling against what God has instituted, and those who do so will bring judgment on themselves."* Romans 13:1-2 (NIV)

The word "submit" in the scriptural passage is from the Greek *hupertasso* which means to arrange self under, to align oneself under the established authority[2]. Conversely, the word "rebel" comes from the Greek word *antitasso* meaning to arrange self against[3]. What a contrary position! All creatures of God must respond to God's established laws and order by either submitting to it or resisting it. Whatever position we take, there will be consequences of gains or pains.

Assuredly, the spirit world recognizes all the authority relationships that God established and yields to the lawful exercise of that authority. This explains why demonic spirits can see the spiritual condition of any individual and identify any legal grounds to attack (See Matthew 12:43; Acts 19). Knowing this should keep us believers on our toes.

Human beings, nevertheless, can yield the authority over their lives either to God, or Satan, by the exercise of their free will and choice. The Scripture puts this succinctly in the following words by the apostle Paul in one of his epistles: *"Don't you know that when you offer yourselves to someone to obey him as slaves, you are slaves to the one whom you obey -- whether you are slaves to sin, which leads to death, or to obedience, which leads to righteousness?"* Romans 6:14 (NIV).

From the Scripture above, we see that allegiance or obedience to either God or Satan increases the authority and power of God or Satan in the life of the individual. The more we obey God or Satan, the more their power and influence or stronghold is established over our lives. So if I want God's influence and power to be fully operational for me to experience increase in my life, I have to keep in the path of obeying Him.

Interestingly, whatever a leader does with his authority affects every person under his care. Adam, in the fall, gave us all over to the authority of Satan. *"And he said to him 'I will give you all their authority and splendor, for it has been given to me, and I can give it to anyone I want to'"* Luke 4:6 (NIV). Conversely, Jesus, in His vicarious death, restored all who believe in Him back to God. *"So Christ was once offered to bear the sins of many; and unto them that look for him shall he appear the second time without sin unto salvation"* Hebrews 9:28 (KJV).

Accordingly, when a person yields his authority to Satan, Satan uses it against a person from one generation to another. We are still suffering the consequences of Adam's yield of authority to Satan today. Certainly, when we fall into Satan's hand like Adam did when he yielded authority, we have ourselves to blame. The Scripture says in Exodus 20:4-6 (ESV) *"You shall not make for yourself a carved image, or any likeness of anything that is in heaven above, or that is in the earth beneath, or that is in the water under the earth; you shall not bow down to them nor serve them. For I, the LORD your God, am a jealous God, visiting the iniquity of the fathers on the children to the third and fourth generations of those who hate Me, but showing mercy to thousands, to those who love Me and keep My commandments."*

Why would God have to say this to His own chosen ones? Because He knows that although He wanted to help them in love, their yielding of authority would make the devil torment them perpetually and generationally. Any commitment, dedication, curse or blessing entered into by a person in one generation may give authority over that person's descendants. It happened with Adam, with Abraham, with David, with Achan, and with Eli. I hope it won't with you! Remember, if the curses and commitments are not canceled, they pass on perpetually from one generation to another. May God help us.

THE HUSBAND IS THE SPIRITUAL GATEKEEPER

In Ephesians 5:23 (NKJV), the Scripture addresses the role of a man in his home and over his family: *"For the husband is head of the wife, as also Christ is head of the church; and He is the Savior of the body."* Now the Scripture is clear as to the extent and degree to which the husband is to provide protection for the wife. It says "as," meaning in just the same manner as Christ did for the church.

The husband is the savior of the body, in his case the family, and as such he is to deliver it, protect, it and make it safe. The role of husband being the savior of the body is likened to Jesus being the Savior of His body, the church. You and I know what it cost Him to deliver it, and what it has taken Him for 2000 years to protect continually and keep it safe from satanic vandalism.

But in all this, the woman is to be subject and submissive to her husband. By doing this, she places herself in battle under the leadership direction of her husband so as to flow as a team and fulfill the purpose God intended for the man. It is equally important to note that order in family relationship precedes spiritual warfare in Ephesians 6. Any woman who has properly taken her place under the leadership authority of her husband is a terror to the kingdom of darkness for it is dismayed by her alignment to do battle on solid ground.

A GATEKEEPER CONTROLS THE ENTRANCE

The gate is very strategic in spiritual warfare because the gate is the entrance to any city. The moment an enemy takes the gate of a city, it has taken the city. No wonder the Scripture says of the descendants of Abraham that they shall possess the gate of their enemies (See Genesis 22:17). Take the gate, take the city.

The Scripture makes it clear that the gate is the place of entrance and of authority. *"And I also say to you that you are Peter, and on this rock I will build My church, and the gates of Hades shall not prevail against it. And I will give you the keys of the kingdom of heaven, and whatever you bind on earth will be bound in heaven, and whatever you loose on earth will be loosed in heaven"* Matthew 16:18-19 (NKJV).

In the Old Testament, the Scripture depicts the elders sitting at the gates of the city making decisions and exercising authority. That is serious! If the husband is the elder of his family and head of authority, then any spiritual influences that enter the family come as a result of the exercise of his authority. He, the man and head of the family, can allow demonic activity or allow Holy Spirit activity, as the case may be, by the exercise of his authority for whatever he allows and permits in the family stays and holds.

Ideally, the man has greater authority and greater responsibilities in the family. He is assigned the task of protecting those weaker and more vulnerable to demonic onslaught. But in doing this, he must not take advantage of them either at home or in the church.

Moreover, the key principle to exercising authority is service, motivated by love the purpose of which is to protect, to bless and to nurture.

> *Jesus called them together and said, "You know that the rulers of the Gentiles lord it over them, and their high officials exercise authority over them. Not so with you. Instead, whoever wants to become great among you must be your servant, and whoever wants to be first must be your slave -- just as the Son of Man did not come to be served, but to serve, and to give his life as a ransom for many."* Matthew 20:25-28 (NIV)

PROTECT YOUR HOME

The Scripture says in 1 Timothy 5:8 that *"If anyone does not provide for his relatives, and especially for his immediate family, he has denied the faith and is worse than an unbeliever."* So how then can a husband provide around protection, spiritual, financial, natural and much more for his family? He does this by fully assuming his God-given responsibilities and exercising authority in love over his family.

The husband must first and foremost provide spiritually for his family by way of enhancing and ensuring their personal relationship with Christ, holding his wife and children in heart, and exercising spiritual authority.

The husband is to connect the family to Christ, receive guidance for them and then resolve personal issues that bother every member of the family accordingly. Every man and husband must note that the spiritual temperature of his family relationship with God is set in motion and determined by him.

The first thing that comes to every thinking man when he is ready for marriage is that he is in for responsibility. He has to take the responsibility, spiritual, financial, and otherwise, first and foremost of the wife and then of the children. And he is to do this with joy and not with heavy heart or as grievous burden.

Also as a priest over his own house, he is to take over completely the spiritual atmosphere of his home by speaking into the spirit world to forbid and release any member of his family from sin. He is to break off spiritual attacks on his wife and then off of his children. He is to create a future in the realm of the spirit by releasing faith-filled words into the future and into the lives of the children before and after they are born.

Also, in the natural physical world, the husband has a lot of commitments and responsibilities to perform for his wife and for all the members of his family, individually and collectively.

He is to hold fast his covenant commitment to his wife, seek to keep her secure and stay in complete unity with her at all time cost. *"But did He not make them one, having a remnant of the Spirit? And why one? He seeks godly offspring. Therefore take heed to your spirit, And let none deal treacherously with the wife of his youth"* Malachi 2:15 (NKJV).

The wise husband listens to his wife's needs and concerns, attending to her need of loneliness. He seeks to lift the wife out of loneliness with comfort and cheerfulness. *"Husbands, likewise, dwell with them with understanding, giving honor to the wife, as to the weaker vessel, and as being heirs together of the grace of life, that your prayers may not be hindered"* 1 Peter 3:7 (NKJV).

The husband is under a heavenly loving obligation to honor, affirm and value his wife. This way, he cures the wife of low self-esteem. In his book, "The 5 Love Languages", Gary Chapman reveals that one love language that helps to build self-esteem in people, husbands or wives, are words of affirmation[4] (See 1 Pet 3:7).

It is the husband's responsibility to give direction at home. It is his responsibility to create, set and establish Christian family values for the entire family to follow as a standard. It is his responsibility to assign responsibilities and help to prioritize the activities of the home. In doing these things, he is, to a large extent, taking the burden of running the home off the wife. *"But as for me and my house, we will serve the LORD"* Joshua 24:15 (ESV).

Wherever there are two or more people, there is bound to be disagreement and sometimes frictions and disunity. It is the husband's responsibility to ensure that unity and agreement are part of his home. He must choose to exercise and foster unity, knowing full well that where there is disagreement, disunity, and strife, there is all manner of evil. *"Every kingdom divided against itself will be ruined, and every city or household divided against itself will not stand."* (Matthew 12:25 (NIV). See also Psalm 133; Matthew 18:19.

EXERCISE YOUR SPIRITUAL AUTHORITY

What use is the knowledge of authority if we do not know how to exercise it? The ultimate purpose of these studies about battles is to inform us of the realities of life and have us come to the knowledge of who we are in God. Then standing on the vantage point of authority, bring the kingdom of God to bear in our world. We are people of authority; we must use it otherwise it has no purpose.

In understanding how to exercise authority, we have to look and take a hint from the Person *who set authority in place and learn from Him how He exercised it. "They were all amazed and spoke among themselves, saying, 'What a word this is!' For with authority and power He commands the unclean spirits and they come out"* Luke 4:36 (NKJV).

In this Scripture, we see Jesus had just cast out an unclean spirit from a man through exercising His spiritual authority. The people of His day were amazed by the way He issued commands and by the fact that the demons not once could challenge Him. Jesus understood authority, used and exercised it justly.

According to the Strong's Concordance, the word "authority" comes from the Greek word *exousia* that means the power of rule or government; the delegated legal right to speak and act on behalf of a King[5]. Authority is a delegated and legal right to speak or to initiate action. I like that. For example, a policeman in uniform has a delegated right to speak and act on behalf of the government of his nation. With that authority vested in him, he can initiate actions for and against a person or thing.

The word "power" is derived from the Greek word *dunamis* which means the supernatural strength and ability to carry out a task[6]. Simply put, authority is the right to do, while power is the ability to do. We see Jesus exercise both in His life and ministry.

We know that delegated authority must be from one person of higher influence and superiority to one who is a subordinate or an under-ruler. Jesus received His authority from His Heavenly Father, as part of His commission and through intimacy and obedience continually to the Father, He maintained this authority and power (See John 5:19).

More unique and captivating is the way Jesus exercised this authority; He used a strong, forceful verbal command: *"Be quiet and come out of him,"* Jesus said to the demon in the demon possessed man Luke 4:35 (NKJV). Authority is exercised through forceful verbal declaration and command of the Word of God and power is demonstrated through the Holy Spirit within. This was how Jesus exercised His authority and power. We know that the power Jesus demonstrated was the Holy Spirit flowing through Him. *"But if I cast out demons by the Spirit of God, surely the kingdom of God has come upon you"* Matthew 12:28 (NKJV).

What Jesus Accomplished on Our Behalf

Now for us to fully grasp the exercise of authority Jesus used, we must first and foremost understand what Jesus accomplished for us through His substitutional death on the cross for humanity.

> *And you, being dead in your trespasses and the uncircumcision of your flesh, He has made alive together with Him, having forgiven you all trespasses, having wiped out the handwriting of requirements that was against us, which was contrary to us. And He has taken it out of the way, having nailed it to the cross. Having disarmed principalities and powers, He made a public spectacle of them, triumphing over them in it.* Colossians 2:13-15 (NKJ)

Knowing full well that the question of authority and the exercise of it by humans was lost to the devil at the fall of Adam in the Garden, God had to, through Jesus as our representative, settle with the usurper, the devil and disarm all the spiritual principalities and the power of death by way of Jesus' death on the cross.

We see Jesus before His death on the cross through His walk of obedience to the Father overcome every assault of Satan against Him. Ultimately, on the cross Jesus acted as the representative of all mankind and disarmed all spiritual principalities and powers by His death and resurrection. The only way to have authority over another is first to take from the person in authority his staff of authority and then empower another person being elevated to that position of authority with the same staff of authority. This was what Jesus did for us in His death, burial, and resurrection. He had to take from Satan the authority he was currently exercising over humanity and when He rose from the dead, He vested that authority in the new creation and redeemed man, in as many who believe in His name.

Let us examine the key words in the verse of Scripture quoted above from Colossians 2:14-15. The word "disarmed" from the Strong's

Exhaustive Concordance of the New Testament means to strip off all clothes or weapons and to totally put off[7]. Is this what Jesus did when He met Satan and all his hosts in open combat in hell in His death?

The word "triumph" in this verse according to the Strong's Concordance means to celebrate a complete and decisive victory over one's enemies[8]. Isn't that what the resurrection of Jesus Christ from the dead is all about? Is it not about the celebration of the triumph of life over darkness, of heaven over hell, and of God over Satan for all time and eternity? We are assured and are confident that Jesus' victory at the cross caused a complete transfer of spiritual authority to take place from those defeated to the triumphant conqueror.

On the cross, Satan lost all the "legal rights" over humanity that Adam had surrendered to him in the Garden. Now all authority in heaven and earth legally belongs to Jesus as the triumphant Victor and the Champion of Humanity (See Matthew 28:18). And let us not forget that Jesus was God's representative man on the behalf of humanity. What Jesus did, He did for us. The victory and triumph He gained over the old archenemy are ours. Hallelujah!

At the cross, Jesus legally broke the power of sin completely according to Colossians 2:14 (NIV): *"having canceled the written code, with its regulations, that was against us and that stood opposed to us; he took it away, nailing it to the cross."* But He did not stop there. He also broke the power of curses that day. No curse has any right to attach itself and to work its evil forebodings in the life of a Christian. We have been released instead into the blessing, to live and to walk in it. Christ has redeemed us from the curse of the law, having become a curse for us for it is written, *"Cursed is everyone who hangs on a tree, that the blessing of Abraham might come upon the Gentiles in Christ Jesus, that we might receive the promise of the Spirit through faith"* Galatians 3:13-14 (NKJV).

Moreover, through the cross, Jesus legally broke completely the power of griefs (sicknesses) and trauma (pains and torments): *"Surely he has borne our griefs and carried our sorrows; yet we esteemed him stricken, smitten by God, and afflicted."* Isaiah 53:4 (ESV). He also did not spare sickness: *"But he was wounded for our transgressions; he was crushed for our iniquities; upon him was the chastisement that brought us peace, and with his stripes we are healed"* Isaiah 53:5 (ESV).

Ultimately, Jesus through the cross broke completely legally and forever the power and hold of iniquity by the one and only all-sufficient sacrifice of Himself. *"All we like sheep have gone astray; we have turned every one to his own way; and the LORD has laid on him the iniquity of us all"* Isaiah 53:6 (ESV). Now we are liberated legally once and for all time. Our territories are liberated for time and eternity. We have to march straight onto the battlefront with our banner of victory hoisted over our heads. Jesus is King and Victor; we are the armies of the Conqueror. Hallelujah!

Today, those who believe and are followers of Christ, who are joined to His Spirit and abiding in Him, are raised to a new level to share with Him in His victory and authority only through faith. We have been given legally delegated authority to speak and act on His behalf to advance His Kingdom. But it is a pity that in spite of the cross, a majority of people including Christians still give the devil legal rights to enter and manipulate their lives. This ought not be the lot of an intelligent child of God.

YOUR GIVEN SPIRITUAL AUTHORITY

Behold, I give you the authority (exousia) to trample on serpents and scorpions, and over all the power (dunamis) of the enemy and nothing shall by any means hurt you." Luke 10:19 (NKJV)

We have just seen what Jesus accomplished for us on the cross, the ultimate defeat of the devil and the recovery of man's lost authority back to him. Now we want to see how Jesus restored the authority back to the redeemed man and then clothed him with the responsibility of exercising it on His behalf.

Let's look at the seventy disciples that Jesus sent forth into the towns and villages that He was about to visit. Jesus, was responding to testimonies of these seventy disciples of their dominion over demons and their powers.

Jesus said to them, *"Behold, I give you authority."* That means Jesus gave them "the power and right to command or to exercise force" according to the Strong's Exhaustive Concordance of the New Testament definition of authority[9].

Jesus then added: *"to trample on serpents and scorpions."* Serpent and scorpions are symbols of evil spirits and demonic powers, all the powers and forces of the kingdom of darkness. Jesus identifies these serpents and scorpions as our enemy, ones that hate and desire to hurt us. But God has given us, every believer individually, spiritual authority to exercise dominion over them and to keep them bound and off our territories.

For us to fully enjoy the exercise of this authority to its maximum capacity, we must know that spiritual authority flows out of our status, or standing, with God. We have said over and over again that the knowledge of our identity is key to walking in power and dominion with God. And chief among this knowledge is the knowledge of our righteousness, our right standing with God. We must have a revelation of righteousness to be able to exercise our rights and authority in Christ.

In righteousness, we are set right with God and set free from the hold and control of the devil. We stand justified with God through the finished work of Christ. We have gone to court and have been cleared. Our case is settled, and there is nothing standing between God and us anymore. Our souls have been cleared of guilt and now we stand tall and strong as sons and daughters of God with no spiritual inferiority complex and fear. Sin consciousness that made us weak and helpless before Satan has been taken away and completely eroded by the blood of the cross of Christ. We are no longer cowards and helpless before God and before Satan. This kind of knowledge is the knowledge that empowers the dominion and exercise of authority. Righteousness empowers. *"Therefore, having been justified by faith, we have peace with God through our Lord Jesus Christ, through whom also we have access by faith into this grace in which we stand, and rejoice in hope of the glory of God"* Romans 5:1-2 (NKJV).

To continue to stay in the place of power with God, we must keep our relationship and fellowship with heaven intact. The strength of spiritual authority is fellowship. In fellowship, we are always in touch with heaven, in talking with the Father through the Holy Spirit and in the name of Jesus. A broken fellowship results in power leak so we have to stay connected at all times and stay away from sin that mars our fellowship with God.

A daily visit with the Lord, where our strength is renewed, our fire poured anew, is consistent with a life of power and authority in the realm of the spirit. You cannot stay in touch and fellowship with the Father and not be affected with His presence which is dangerous to demons and devils. We carry from the presence of God the very presence of God when we stay in constant daily fellowship with Him. No wonder Jesus said to His followers, you and me, in John 15:5 (NJKV): *"I am the vine, you are the branches. He who abides in Me, and I in him, bears much fruit; for without Me you can do nothing."* Every branch has to stay on the vine to remain useful, productive and functional.

We also need to yield, by faith, to the power of the Holy Spirit. The Holy Spirit of God is the executive of the Godhead on the earth. He is the custodian of the power and presence of God on the earth. He is the one that fills us with power and faith for the effective exercise of spiritual authority. Our usefulness in this business of exercising authority and dominion over the power of the devil is greatly affected and enhanced when we learn to walk in cooperation with Him, yielding our all to Him and following His leading.

We know that Jesus and the disciples did not just go around casting out demons from every person on the street in their own power, but were dependent on the Holy Spirit's leading and moving to get the job done. Even Paul would and could not do the work of ministry in certain places because the Holy Spirit, whom he had learned to yield to, stopped him from going to those places at times. We are most effective when we let the Holy Spirit guide and lead the way in our life. Yield to Him. *"But if I cast out demons by the Spirit of God, surely the kingdom of God has come upon you"* Matthew 12:28 (NKJV).

INSIGHTS ON THE BELIEVER'S AUTHORITY

We must know that we do not own spiritual authority. It is not the private property of any one Christian such that we can monopolize and use at will to serve our own selfish purpose. This is why we must depend on the Holy Spirit for His use and guidance; otherwise, we might be acting from the flesh. Please let us get it straight from the onset: spiritual authority is a trust from God to us; it is an entrustment from Him and so we have to approach it reverently with all caution.

Jesus Himself understood this and responded to it in the following words: *"For I have come down from heaven, not to do My own will, but the will of Him who sent Me"* John 6:38 (NKJV).

Secondly, since we know that spiritual authority is a trust from God to us, we would then do ourselves good to learn to use it properly for the purpose for which it was given. When the purpose of something is not known, abuse is inevitable. So what is the purpose of spiritual authority? Its purpose is to bring judgment on the evil powers and personalities that are cause torment in the lives of millions and to establish the kingdom of God in their lives. Spiritual authority is for the liberation of humanity from the hold and wickedness of Satan.

Paul put it this way: *"Therefore I write these things being absent, lest being present I should use sharpness, according to the authority which the Lord has given me for edification and not for destruction"* 2 Corinthians 13:10 (NJKV). Paul emphasized edification and not destruction. We are not given power and authority to destroy, use, manipulate and to take advantage of people, but to build them up in purpose and in the counsel of God.

Thirdly, in the exercise of spiritual authority, we must not presume, take for granted, and act out of pride or independence. This thing is about God and you, a vine and branch relationship. God will never accommodate independence which is tantamount to rebellion.

At every instance of the exercise of authority, the Holy Spirit must lead the way, and God must get the glory in the long run. Not you and not your church. God has never, and will not start today, shared His glory with anyone. Let us look at the Scripture and see how Jesus interpreted this kind of attitude. *"Not everyone who says to me, 'Lord, Lord,' will enter the kingdom of heaven, but only he who does the will of my Father who is in heaven. Many will say to me on that day, 'Lord, Lord, did we not prophesy in your name, and in your name drive out demons and perform many miracles?' Then I will tell them plainly, 'I never knew you. Away from me, you evildoers!'"* Matthew 7:21-23 (NIV). I think that is clear enough for everyone that might be prone to presumption, pride, and independence in the exercise of spiritual authority.

Fourthly, for everything that God entrusts to us, He will call for an accounting in the long run. We are accountable to God, who gives us this authority. It is like this: if the government gives you funds to do a community project for the benefit of the people, at the end of the day, you will have to complete the project and provide a written explanation as to how the money was expended down to the last penny. I believe the government learned accountability from God.

Let us take caution as to what we do and how we do what we do (the motive) with what God gave us. He will ask for an explanation in due time. *"So then, each of us will give an account of himself to God."* Romans 14:12 (NIV)

What You have Authority to Do

"Most assuredly I say unto you, he who believes in me, the works that I do he will do also; and greater works than these will he do, because I go to My Father." John 14:12 (NKJV)

If God has entrusted you with authority and you also know that you will have to account for it at the end of time, to what extent are you supposed to use this authority, and how far can you go before you are infringing on God's right and glory that He never shares with anyone?

The answer is Jesus entrusted you, a believer, with His authority and power to do the supernatural works that He did. In the scriptural passage above, Jesus said, *"The works that I do, you are to do and even much more."* From Jesus' statement, we see the sphere of our authority. We are called by Christ to do the same works that He did.

A look at the gospels, Matthew, Mark, Luke, and John, gives us a picture of all that Jesus did and what we are to copy and do. They also told how us He did them. Take the time to read through the gospels. Make up your mind to exercise the authority entrusted you as a member of God's family, doing what Jesus did, the same way He did it.

The Bible is dotted with many things that Jesus did and how He did them. God gave us authority to act as a representative of Jesus and to:

1. Preach the Gospel (Matthew 28:18-19)
2. Make Disciples (Matthew 28:18-19)
3. Bless (Speak empowered words) (Matthew 10:12-13)
4. Break Bondages (Isaiah 10:27)

5. Break Curses (Matthew 16:19)
6. Cast out Demons (Matthew 10:8)
7. Authority to Heal the Sick (Matthew 10:8)
8. Raise the Dead (Matthew 10:8)
9. Bind and Loose (Matthew 16:19)
10. Forgive (John 20:23)

KEYS TO EXERCISING SPIRITUAL AUTHORITY

The Bible is a book of principles that if practiced will produce intended results. This is true for any subject in the Scripture in addition to matters of spiritual authority. For us to walk in the authority God has given us, we need to learn how to use the authority.

The first principle for exercising spiritual authority is faith. We know that faith is the beginning point of our walk with God, *"for without it is impossible to please God"* Hebrews 11:6 (NJKV). With spiritual authority, it is faith in who we are, and in our standing with God.

The Scripture says: *"For you did not receive the spirit of bondage again to fear; but you received the Spirit of adoption by whom we cry out, 'Abba, Father.' The Spirit Himself bears witness with our spirit that we are children of God"* Romans 8:15-16 (NKJV).

Our authority flows out of the position that God has given us in Christ. We should know that position and stay in it. More so, spiritual authority is part of who we are, and it is part of who God says we are. In the kingdom of God, being is more than having. Your person in Christ determines your doing in Christ so take the time to know who you are and then, from that standpoint, you can wield spiritual authority.

Spiritual authority is confirmed to us by virtue of our birth into Christ. You cannot be anything else but royalty if you were born into a King's family. You carry authority in the spirit realm because you are a child of God, a member of His royal family. Hence, to exercise spiritual authority, we must be confident in who we are, we must know that we are sons and daughters of the King!

The second principle to effectively exercise spiritual authority is humility. With humility you learn to position yourself under authority. The Scripture says: *"Therefore submit to God. Resist the devil and he will flee from you"* James 4:7 (NKJV). Submission is key to prevailing in spiritual warfare. When you submit to God and everyone of His constituted authority, you can resist and put the devil to flight any day and anytime.

According to the Strong's Concordance the word "submit" means "to place yourself under the authority of a superior officer so as to work together to gain a military victory[10]." Therefore, submission is an attitude of humility that recognizes and yields to the authority of God and to those He has delegated authority to. By submission, we position ourselves under the authority and direction of the Holy Spirit who enables us to move in God's authority. Conversely, we are to resist and stand against, oppose, and withstand the devil which we can do when our submission to God is in place. Submission to God produces the necessary and an equal resistance to the devil. The measure to which we submit to God determines the measure to which we can put the devil to flight through our resistance.

There is a beautiful story in the Scripture that depicts what authority is and how it operates. It was a statement made by a Roman centurion, a soldier, to Jesus about healing his sick servant when Jesus asked if He should go with the centurion. *"The centurion replied, 'Lord, I do not deserve to have you come under my roof. But just say the word, and my servant will be healed. For I myself am a man under authority, with soldiers under me. I tell this one, 'Go,' and he goes; and that one, 'Come,' and he comes. I say to my servant, "Do this,' and he does it'"* Matthew 8:8-10 (NIV). What a beautiful picture and explanation of submission this humble soldier gives. Jesus healed his servant on the spot.

By design, God requires us to submit to His Word and then grow in faith through that Word to take authority and exercise it.

Another principle to exercising authority is listening to the voice of God.

> *Then Jesus answered and said to them, "Most assuredly, I say to you, the Son can do nothing of Himself, but what He sees the Father do; for whatever he does, the Son also does in like manner. For the Father loves the Son, and shows Him all things that He Himself does; and He will show Him greater works than these, that you may marvel."* John 5:19-20 (NKJV)

Jesus knew this secret more than anyone else even though He was the eternal Son of God. He knew the only thing God is committed to doing is the thing He said He is going to do. Jesus knew that He could not act outside of God's instructions and get results, so He was committed to letting the Father tell Him what to do before doing it. I think this kind of attitude and knowledge will save us a lot of disappointment and failure.

From the verse above, we can deduce that Jesus' authority flowed out of His position as a Son, and also out of personal intimacy, reverence and obedience to the Father. He never presumed or acted independently of the Father both in the things he said and in the things He did. *"I do what I see my Father do,"* He said; *"I speak what my Father tells me to say,"* He commented. His was a complete submission to the Father to doing the things that pleased Him. *"And He who sent Me is with Me. The Father has not left Me alone, for I always do those things that please Him"* John 8:29 (NKJV).

From the life of Jesus, we learn that as we have fellowship and develop deep intimacy with God, our authority grows and increases. Simply put, fellowship with the Father fuels our authority and the ability to exercise it. It is to our best interest to stay in the place of fellowship with the Father where His voice is simple to access. Earthly fathers don't shout instructions on their children in the streets; they do so in the secret of their chambers, in their parlors and in the home. God is not different.

Therefore, it is important we know that to exercise authority on behalf of God, we must know what God wants to accomplish. We cannot exercise God's authority outside of His will. No man who dares to do so will have the full backing of heaven. Why should God furnish you with ability when God knows you are not going to use it for what He wants? And we know what God wants: He wants the kingdom, He wants the glory, and He wants the power. He wants all people, and all demons in hell, to know that Jesus is Lord.

Use Your Voice

The complete and full exercise of our spiritual authority requires the use of our mouth. It requires the use of our tongue, one of the littlest members of the body to take dominion and to exercise spiritual authority. It is about physical strength and fighting and shaking; it is about learning to shoot the weapons of God's Word through our mouths on target.

According to the Scripture, the mouth, "*stoma*" in Greek, is described as "the front or edge of a weapon[11]." It is compared to a sword. We know that a sword is a piece of metal with a handle and two sharp edges with which it does its work. The mouth is like that; it is the edge of a weapon. With it, we take the Sword of the Spirit and wield it in spiritual warfare. The Word of God declared and proclaimed from our mouths is the weapon. Our mouth and our tongue are the instruments that release the weapon.

In Revelation 19:15, 21, we see the Word of God coming forth as a weapon from the mouth of Jesus to strike the nations and to destroy His opposition. Faith-filled words are the weapons with which we exercise spiritual authority while our tongue is the instrument that we use in doing so.

In Mark 11:22-23 (NJKV), we see Jesus giving the disciples this secret of faith-filled power words in the exercise of spiritual authority. The day before, they saw Jesus speak to a tree that refused to bear fruit and the next day something happened to the tree. What Jesus said to the tree happened; it died. The disciples wanted to know what was behind what Jesus did. *"So Jesus answered and said to them, "Have faith in God. For assuredly, I say to you, whoever says to this mountain, 'Be removed and be cast into the sea,' and does not doubt in his heart, but believes that those things he says will be done, he will have whatever he says."*

Jesus' response to their question proved to them that the entire invisible spirit world is listening and would obey the voice of faith when His words are directed toward it. To assert authority, we must do it vocally, by issuing a command, by releasing an order. There is no place for a closed mouth in the exercise of spiritual authority. We cannot think the word to release spiritual authority. It is a command, speaking, talking, saying and expecting what you said or commanded to happen. That's where faith comes in.

From the Webster's Dictionary, we find out that the word "command" means to "issue an order with expectation that it will be carried out[12]." No military general gives an order and expects a subordinate to ignore it because of the way the military is structured; one must obey the last order of a superior officer or obey before complaining.

This is true as the spirit world is also structured. It cannot turn deaf ears to commands and orders from heaven's ambassadors. The spirit world cannot turn a deaf ear to the commands of God's anointed servants who are speaking and acting on God's behalf. No never! It is programmed, structured and under obligation to hear, listen and to obey God's command from our mouths.

All through the ministry of Jesus as recorded in the gospels, we see Jesus simply issuing commands, and sicknesses, demons, winds, trees, and the dead obey Him.

To the sick, He said: *"I am willing; be cleansed."* Immediately the leprosy was cleansed. (See Matthew 8:3; Luke 4:39).

To the demon possessed, He said: *"'Deaf and dumb spirit, I command you, come out of him and enter him no more!' Then the spirit cried out, convulsed him greatly, and came out of him"* Mark 9:25-26 (NKJV).

To the wind and the storm, He spoke: *"Then He arose and rebuked the wind, and said to the sea, 'Peace, be still!' And the wind ceased and there was a great calm"* Mark 4:39; Luke 8:24 (NKJV).

To the trees, *"He spoke: 'Let no one eat fruit from you ever again.' And His disciples heard it... they saw the fig tree dried up from the roots"* Mark 11:14, 20 (NKJV).

And what about dead people? To them He spoke: *"Young man, I say to you, arise"* Luke 7:14 (NKJV). And *"Lazarus, come out!"* John 11:43 (NIV).

That was the way Jesus did it and that is the way we are to do it today. The spirit world is programmed and under obligation to hear and to obey God's Word and voice coming through our mouths.

SPEAK WITH BOLDNESS

It is enough and great to know that God's Word declared through our mouths is the way and weapon by which we exercise spiritual authority. But it is much more important that we know there is a level of confidence that must accompany our words before evil spiritual powers will obey us. Did you know that devils know when you are not sure of yourself and are afraid? They have a spiritual sense to know a confident, convincing command from a weak, fearful and unsure command. Paul knew.

> *And this she did for many days. But Paul, greatly annoyed, turned and said to the spirit, 'I command you in the name of Jesus Christ to come out of her.' And he came out that very hour.* Acts 16:18 (NJKV)

Paul knew that confidence and a convincing command in the name of Jesus would bring the desired result. He knew what the term "in the Name of Jesus' meant. He knew it meant that one is acting as Jesus' personal representative upon the earth. It means that you are acting directly under His authority, you are doing what He requires to be done; you are bringing Heaven to earth as God's ambassador.

To some people, this might seem like a magic wand, but it is not. It is not some 'magic formula' for power to flow. No! It is you speaking as the representative of Jesus as He would speak, forcefully, convincingly and powerfully.

ACTIVATE YOUR FAITH

Lastly on the principles to exercising spiritual authority, we must learn the power of active faith. That means that we must learn and know to expect a response to our commands. We don't just give commands because everybody is doing it, without really expecting anything. It is inconsistent with the nature of the Word of God to say a thing and not expect it to happen. God watches over His Word to perform it. That was not how Jesus did it. That was not how Paul and Peter did it.

> *Have faith in God. For assuredly, I say to you, whoever says to this mountain, 'Be removed and be cast into the sea,' and does not doubt in his heart, but believes that those things he says will be done, he will have whatever he says. Therefore I say to you, whatever things you ask when you pray, believe that you receive them, and you will have them.* Mark 11: 22-24 (NKJV)

From the life of Christ, we see that commanding must be forceful, strong, and must flow from within our recreated spirit man. The river that flows from our bellies, our hearts, is the source that will get the job done, not the one from our head.

More so, spiritual kingdoms are enforced by spirits that ride upon, or are activated, by words spoken by someone with authority to do so. But the person must do so with no doubt in his or her heart. He must do so with a confident expectation that the words he or she speaks carry weight and will be heard and responded to by the spirits. By the way, there are no idle words in the realm of the spirit. They are either obeyed or ignored as the case may be depending on who is issuing the command.

God's Word is more than sounds and sentences; it is not mere words. It describes reality. Even in the mouth of a child in faith, God's Word can work wonders. This is why the Scripture says that: *"Out of the mouth of babes and nursing infants You have ordained strength, Because of Your enemies, That You may silence the enemy and the avenger"* Psalm 8:2 (NKJV).

God's Word is not ordinary. It has the power to demolish kingdoms and barriers no matter who, young or old, male or female, is declaring it. It must, however, come out of a heart of faith. The words you speak must be empowered by faith from your heart or they may end up just being sounds and noises. God never intend this.

Did Peter, Paul and the apostles know this truth? I trust they did.. Peter issued a command to a man who born lame saying: *"In the Name of Jesus Christ rise up and walk"* Acts 3:6 (NKJV) and he walked. What about Paul? He *"... said with a loud voice 'stand up straight on your feet' ..."* Acts 14:10 (NJKV), and the man who was lame on his feet from birth stood up and walked home.

And again Paul said: *"to the spirit I command you in the Name of Jesus Christ come out of him'"* Acts 16:18 (NJKV). The girl with the spirit of divination lost the spirit at the instance of the command of faith and boldness from the mouth of anointed and commissioned ambassador Paul. And Peter: *"turning to the body and said, 'Tabitha, arise!' And she opened her eyes"* Acts 9:40 (NJKV). That was the climax of Peter's miracle ministry as recorded in the book of Acts. Tabitha, who was dead and prepared for burial, came back to life.

Has God changed? No. *"Jesus Christ is the same yesterday and today and forever."* Hebrews 13:8 (NIV). Let us dare to do what Jesus and the disciples did, the same way they did it. *"For there is no distinction between Jew and Greek, for the same Lord over all is rich to all who call upon Him"* Romans 10:12 (NKJ V).

CHAPTER TWENTY - BATTLE PLAN

We have gone over a lot in this book. From understanding our enemy, learning from great battles in the Old Testament, to taking our rightful position in God's army as kings, and arising and understanding our authority in Jesus Christ.

Now it's time to take all this knowledge and put it into practice.

ANOINTED BY THE HOLY SPIRIT

But you shall receive power when the Holy Spirit has come upon you; and you shall be witnesses to Me in Jerusalem, and in all Judea and Samaria, and to the end of the earth. Acts 1:8 (NJKV)

Jesus promised to "anoint" us with the Holy Spirit. The anointing is an empowerment to accomplish the apostolic mandate. The power of the Holy Spirit enables you to fulfill the assignment God has given you to go, preach, heal the sick, and cast out demons. You must receive instruction from the Father the same way Jesus did, and exercise authority and dominion over the things the Holy Spirit instructs you to do.

Governing Your Spiritual Territory

But the manifestation of the Spirit is given to each one for the profit of all. 1 Corinthians 12:7 (NJKV)

Every believer is given something that will advance the Kingdom of God. We are called to be an ambassador of heaven on earth and are given the ability to manifest the life and power of the Spirit of God. Realize that you are equipped and prepared for the apostolic ministry.

"We, however, will not boast beyond measure, but within the limits of the sphere which God appointed us — a sphere which especially includes you. For we are not overextending ourselves (as though our authority did not extend to you), for it was to you that we came with the gospel of Christ; not boasting of things beyond measure, that is, in other men's labors, but having hope, that as your faith is increased, we shall be greatly enlarged by you in our sphere, to preach the gospel in the regions beyond you, and not to boast in another man's sphere of accomplishment." 2 Corinthians 10:13 (NKJV)

Each one of us has been given a ministry assignment through the Holy Spirit. Your territory has been measured out for you by God. It is your assignment and responsibility to have authority over a physical place, or a position of responsibility, or a group of people. The Lord measures out to you a specific territory in which you can move in power and make the Kingdom of God known.

Paul clearly recognized his territory and the areas of assignment and responsibility that was measured out by God to him. It is your responsibility to identify your territory and govern it as kings. Whatever God wants you to take responsibility over is your territory. Seek His purpose and plan to understand what your territory is. Recognize that you are a walking embassy of heaven. Be sure this is reflected in your territory.

Your territory includes the following areas:

- Your mind, will, and emotions
- Your physical body - keep it healthy and fit
- Your relationship with your spouse
- Your family's values, culture, boundaries, and disciplines
- Your home maintenance, management, and hospitality
- The maintenance and management of your possessions
- The development and growth of your ministry
- The relationships, spiritual atmosphere, evangelism of your community
- The spiritual atmosphere and influence of your workplace

Then the LORD God took the man and put him in the Garden of Eden to tend and keep it. Genesis 2:15 (NKJV)

Within your area of influence, your territory, there are two key responsibilities God entrusts to you: to tend which is to work as an act of worship, to cultivate and develop and to keep is to guard which is to watch over, to protect it from an enemy. We are given responsibility to cultivate our territory as a representative of God and to bring the flow of the life and creativity of heaven to earth. We are also required to protect His territory from destruction and invasion by an enemy.

We need not fail in our responsibilities. We must remain vigilant and not become passive in the presence of a spiritual enemy. If we fail to govern and exercise spiritual authority, there may be some devastating consequences.

Failure to exercise spiritual authority could cause damage in your relationship with God and your spouse. You could lose ground and lose spiritual authority to the enemy which can lead to becoming oppressed by the enemy and even causing sickness. Keep it up and the negative consequences of your failure could have a generational impact.

We can see this reflected in the parable Jesus shared about a nobleman going into a far country. As you read this, the nobleman is Jesus Christ. The servants of the nobleman are believers in Christ

> Therefore He said: "A certain nobleman went into a far country to receive for himself a kingdom and to return. So he called ten of his servants, delivered to them ten minas, and said to them, 'Do business till I come.' But his citizens hated him, and sent a delegation after him, saying, 'We will not have this man reign over us.' And so it was that when he returned, having received the kingdom, he then commanded these servants, to whom he had given the money, to be called to him, that he might know how much every man had gained by trading. Then came the first, saying 'Master, your mina has earned ten minas.' And he said to him, 'Well done, good servant; because you were faithful in a very little, have authority over ten cities.'...
>
> "For I say to you that to everyone who has will be given; and from him who does not have, even what he has will be taken away from him" Luke 19:12-17, 26 (NJKV)

As mentioned before, every believer is a servant of the Lord, entrusted to advance the Kingdom of God. God expects every believer to be productive. It is your responsibility to use your talents and abilities to establish order and become productive within your territory.

At the coming of the Lord, every believer will be called to give an account to Him of how productive he or she has been. Believers who have been productive will be commended, and rewarded with increased responsibility and authority. Believers who have failed to be productive will be rebuked and experience loss of opportunity, and authority. God has given us instructions, has taught us how we should live, how we should govern our territory. If we were given all these great talents and treasures but did not use them, I doubt God would be overly happy. God takes pleasure in, and rewards, faith, initiative, and perseverance.

So, how should we govern our territory effectively? It starts with holding your territory in your heart in prayer.

> *And I am sure of this, that he who began a good work in you will bring it to completion at the day of Jesus Christ. It is right for me to feel this way about you all, because I hold you in my heart, for you are all partakers with me of grace, both in my imprisonment and in the defense and confirmation of the gospel.* Phil.1:6-7 (ESV)

Paul held the Philippians in his heart in prayer. He was confident that the Spirit of God would continue to move upon them because he held them in prayer. To hold someone or something in your heart, you must welcome and embrace them in prayer, and assume responsibility to do what God has entrusted you do for them. However, hurts, difficulties, disappointments, distractions and passivity can cause you to let people and responsibilities go out of your heart. When you draw back and fail to engage, spiritual forces enter and operate. Thus, you need to be constantly focusing on God, who can fix the hurts, and forgive those who do you wrong.

The good news is we have a counselor in the Holy Spirit. It is the work of the Holy Spirit to give direction and guidance. Ask for His help. Ask for wisdom. Ask for understanding. And expect a response. He will guide you in your prayer life, as well as in governing your territory.

Gain a clear vision of what is possibly in your territory. God just doesn't give you the territory without giving you a sense of ownership. Imagine what is possible for your territory! Search the Word of God for promises you can take ahold of. Make goals for your family, and for your job. Get creative!

Not only should we envision what our territory should be, but we also need to speak it out and declare it.

> *By faith we understand that the universe was created by the word of God, so that what is seen was not made out of things that are visible.*
> Hebrews 11:3 (ESV)

Subdue any opposing spirits and forbid their operation. Decree that they are subject to the name of Jesus Christ. Speak the Word of God and its promises over your territory. Speaking is great to do in your "war room" or prayer closet, but you also must go out and be physically present and actively engaged in your territory. You cannot be hidden and exert authority from afar. You must be actively engaged in cultivating and developing your territory. You have to build trust with people before you can have access into their lives. God will work and be proactive to all opportunities that arise.

Most important, persevere. Don't yield when unexpected difficulties or resistance arise.

EXERCISING AUTHORITY IN YOUR PERSONAL LIFE

Ephesians 4:27 states to *"give no place to the devil"*. This was written to you and me as believers. The first place to gain victory is over your life. You must recognize the strategies evil spirits use to manipulate and control your life. The word "place" means "opportunity, foothold, legal ground or right[1]". You must close down the "gates" or doors or any legal rights of entrance. Be super vigilant in these areas. What may seem innocent or culturally correct are, in fact, potential opportunities for the enemy to gain access into your life.

The main purpose of this book is to help you be aware of the enemy and aware of his tactics.

> *Lest Satan should take advantage of us for we are not ignorant of his devices.* 2 Corinthians 2:11 (NKJV)

The enemy will deceive you. He will take advantage of the fact that you lack knowledge or information about him or ignored Jesus' teachings as irrelevant, or too difficult to implement.

> *And you He made alive, who were dead in trespasses and sins, 2 in which you once walked according to the course of this world, according to the prince of the power of the air, the spirit who now works in the sons of disobedience."* Ephesians.2:2 (NKJV)

Demonic spirits use legal rights to enter people and to work constantly, using spiritual power or energy, to oppress and destroy them. People experience the negative pressure or energy and think it is just them. Demonic spirits "hold down " people without them realizing the source of the bondage or oppression.

We see these attacks in the following common areas:
- Body – addictions, sickness, weakness, weariness
- Soul – conflict, emotional turmoil, accusation, temptation
- Spirit – heaviness, oppression, passivity
- Finances – unexplained damage, loss, accidents, theft
- Relationships – confusion, offense, misunderstandings
- Circumstances – setbacks, blockages, irritations, accidents

You must learn how to arise, exercise dominion over these areas and break free of any limitation caused by demonic spirits.

I love how after Jesus redeemed Peter, He affirmed His identity, and gave him the power and authority to reign over his life.

> *And I also say to you that you are Peter, and on this rock I will build my church and the gates of hell shall not prevail against it, 19 And I will give you the keys of the kingdom of heaven, and whatever you bind on*

earth will be bound in heaven, and whatever you loose on earth will be loosed in heaven. Matthew 16:18 (NKJV)

Jesus gave Peter, and you, the ability and authority to shut down the enemy; to close the gates. You must understand and claim your identity, your authority, and your power available through the name of Jesus and take control of your life. God has already granted you victory.

> *"You shall not make for yourself a carved image, or any likeness of anything that is in heaven above, or that is in the earth beneath, or that is in the water under the earth. You shall not bow down to them or serve them, for I the Lord your God am a jealous God, visiting the iniquity of the fathers on the children to the third and the fourth generation of those who hate me, but showing steadfast love to thousands of those who love me and keep my commandments."* Exodus 20:4-6 (ESV)

Some of the stuff you need to get rid of may have started before you were born. The after effect, or iniquity, of sin, began in your ancestral line and the consequences were passed down from generation to generation. We saw this with Hezekiah and his father, Ahaz.

Some sins can be passed down to the 3rd or 4th generation. Sexual sins can have an ongoing impact for ten generations according to Deuteronomy 23:2. Sometimes, family lines are weakened and infected with recurring patterns of sin.

Take some time to examine your family tree and ask the Holy Spirit to reveal patterns of sin and failure that appear in other members of your family. Are you under pressure and struggle with these issues too? You have authority to renounce and cancel all generational curses.

> *"They sacrificed their sons and their daughters to the demons"* Psalm 106:37 (ESV)

To dedicate someone is to set apart, to devote to a god, for a special purpose. People from Asian, African, or American Indian ancestry may have been dedicated to false gods and evil spirits as an infant. These ungodly dedications provide a legal right for evil spirits to enter and oppress. You have authority to renounce and to cancel any such dedication.

> *"And his soul was drawn to Dinah the daughter of Jacob. He loved the young woman and spoke tenderly to her."* Genesis 34:3 (ESV)

A soul tie is a bonding or close attachment formed between two people. Soul ties can be godly and have a positive effect on relationships, such as between a husband and wife, or a parent and child. However, whatever can be godly, Satan can use for ungodly purposes. Some soul ties can have a negative impact on your life. A common negative soul tie is having sexual partners before marriage, or blood pacts, or abusive and controlling people. You have authority to renounce and break all ungodly soul ties.

> *Then he touched their eyes, saying, "According to your faith be it done to you."* Matthew 9:29 (ESV)

The things you focus on, what you believe in your heart, influence the course of your life.

There can be judgments or negative expectations often made as a result of painful or bitter experiences. These ungodly beliefs create a doorway for the enemy to operate. You have authority to renounce and cancel all ungodly beliefs and judgments.

> *Like a sparrow in its flitting, like a swallow in its flying, a curse that is causeless does not alight* Proverbs 26:2 (ESV)

A curse is words spoken that release evil spirits to destroy. Using common word curses may originate from parents or close relatives, teachers or authority figures. You can speak negatively over your own life. A common form of self-cursing is a "death wish", i.e. "I just wish I was dead". You have authority to break all such curses. Replace those words with words of life from God's Word.

There may be other items that the Holy Spirit will reveal to you. It's best not try to question it or try to validate it. If it comes to mind, go ahead and take authority against it. Take some time right now.

Pray strongly in tongues for at least ten minutes. Play some worship music and energize your spirit. Get ready to listen for the direction of the Holy Spirit. He will give you direction and revelation.

Then, speak words strongly to confess any personal sin and repent. Release forgiveness to those who have hurt you. Renounce any curse, dedication, vow, soul tie, word curse, or ungodly beliefs. Break any spiritual claims on your life. Cancel their right of access, and command them to go. Then when you are finished, decree a blessing over your life.

As you do this, you may feel a release of pressure or release of a burden; you will feel light and clean inside. Persist until you feel there is total release!

This should become a common and quick practice as you are living in a fallen world. The Lord will continue to mold you and grow you, and revealing deeper convictions for you to address. The Holy Spirit may bring other things to mind later on. Please do not receive them as condemnation. Just know that He desires you to be victorious in all aspects of our life.

Spend time daily in praise and worship. Make sure you discipline your life – stop sinning. Daily, be filled with the Holy Spirit by speaking in tongues and asking Him to fill you with His love.

You have been given an amazing life in Christ. God has given you more than you know. Take your rightful place with Christ at the right hand of the throne of God. Use your power and authority to help bring His Kingdom to earth, in Jesus name.

Take these truths, apply them to your life and live your victorious life now!

REFERENCES

CHAPTER 2 - THE ENEMY

1. Intertestamental period - Wikipedia, the free encyclopedia, https://en.wikipedia.org/wiki/Intertestamental_period (accessed June 07, 2016).
2. "8483 spiritual warfare, causes of" Manser, M. H. (2009). Dictionary of Bible Themes: The Accessible and Comprehensive Tool for Topical Studies. London: Martin Manser.
3. Ibid.

CHAPTER 3 - BATTLEFIELD

1. "counterfeit" Def. 3. counterfeit. Dictionary.com. Dictionary.com Unabridged. Random House, Inc. http://www.dictionary.com/browse/counterfeit (accessed: June 07, 2016).

CHAPTER 4 - ENEMY TACTICS

1. "956 - belos" Strong, J. (1995). Enchanted Strong's Lexicon. Woodside Bible Fellowship.

CHAPTER 5 - STRONGHOLDS

1. Strongholds: What they are and how to pull them down" http://www.transformourworld.org/en/mentoring/stronholds (accessed June 08, 2016)
2. "3053 - logismos" Strong, J. (1995). Enchanted Strong's Lexicon. Woodside Bible Fellowship.

CHAPTER 6 - RESTORING THE FOUNDATION

1. Sermon Illustrations, Quotes, Stories, and Analogies by ..., http://kentcrocket.com/cgi-bin/illustrations/index.cgi?topic=Foundations (accessed June 07, 2016)
2. "1344 - dikaioo" Strong, J. (1995). Enchanted Strong's Lexicon. Woodside Bible Fellowship.

CHAPTER 10 - JERICHO

1. "Moody's Anecdotes and Illustrations", pp. 48-49. Dwight Lyman Moody, Bottom of the Hill Publishing, Sept 01, 2010
2. "pull" Def. 38b. Dictionary.com. Dictionary.com Unabridged. Random House, Inc. http://www.dictionary.com/browse/pull (Accessed: June 09, 2016)
3. "cast" Def 1. Dictionary.com. Dictionary.com Unabridged. Random House, Inc. http://www.dictionary.com/browse/cast (accessed: June 09, 2016)

Chapter 12 - Kings

1. King of Sparta | Bible.org, https://bible.org/illustration/king-sparta (accessed June 07, 2016)

Chapter 13 - Kings & Priests

1. "3259 - ya'ad (meet)" Strong, J. (1995). Enchanted Strong's Lexicon. Woodside Bible Fellowship.

Chapter 14 - Fallen Kings

1. "blame" Def 2. Dictionary.com. Dictionary.com Unabridged. Random House, Inc. http://www.dictionary.com/browse/blame (accessed: June 07, 2016).

Chapter 15 - Stronger

1. "2388 - chazaq (strengthened)" Strong, J. (1995). Enchanted Strong's Lexicon. Woodside Bible Fellowship.
2. "1369 - gabuwrah (might)" Strong, J. (1995). Enchanted Strong's Lexicon. Woodside Bible Fellowship.
3. "confession" Def 2. Dictionary.com. Dictionary.com Unabridged. Random House, Inc. http://www.dictionary.com/browse/blame (accessed: June 07, 2016).
4. "meditate" Merriam-Webster.com. Accessed June 10, 2016. http://www.merriam-webster.com/dictionary/meditate.

Chapter 16 - Prayer

1. "enlarge" Merriam-Webster.com. Accessed June 10, 2016. http://www.merriam-webster.com/dictionary/enlarge.

Chapter 17 - Victory

1. Hell Week | Navy SEALs, http://navyseals.com/nsw/hell-week-0/ (accessed June 07, 2016)
2. "appointed" Merriam-Webster.com. Accessed June 10, 2016. http://www.merriam-webster.com/dictionary/appointed.
3. "apostello" Simmons, W.A. (2014) Calling or Commission. D. Magnum, D.R. Brown, R. Klippenstein, & R. Hurst (Eds.), Lexham Theological Wordbook. Bellingham, WA: Lexham Press
4. "apostle" Smith, C.A (2014) Church Leadership. D. Magnum, D.R. Brown, R. Klippenstein, & R. Hurst (Eds.), Lexham Theological Wordbook. Bellingham, WA: Lexham Press
5. "mandate" Merriam-Webster.com. Accessed June 10, 2016. http://www.merriam-webster.com/dictionary/mandate.

6. "exousia" Merrill, R. (2014) Authority. D. Magnum, D.R. Brown, R. Klippenstein, & R. Hurst (Eds.), Lexham Theological Wordbook. Bellingham, WA: Lexham Press

Chapter 19 - Authority

1. Lighthouse Laws | Bible.org, https://bible.org/illustration/lighthouse-laws (accessed June 07,2016)
2. "5293 - hupotasso" Strong, J. (1995). Enchanted Strong's Lexicon. Woodside Bible Fellowship.
3. "498 - antitasso" Thomas, R. L. (1998). New American Standard Hebrew-Aramaic and Greek dictionaries : updated edition. Anaheim: Foundation Publications, Inc.
4. Chapman, Gary D. 1995. The five love languages: how to express heartfelt commitment to your mate. Chicago: Northfield Pub.
5. "exousia" Merrill, R. (2014) Authority. D. Magnum, D.R. Brown, R. Klippenstein, & R. Hurst (Eds.), Lexham Theological Wordbook. Bellingham, WA: Lexham Press
6. "1411 - dunamis" Thomas, R. L. (1998). New American Standard Hebrew-Aramaic and Greek dictionaries : updated edition. Anaheim: Foundation Publications, Inc.
7. "554 - apekdoumai (disarm)" Strong, J. (1995). Enchanted Strong's Lexicon. Woodside Bible Fellowship.
8. "7321 - rooah (triumph)" Strong, J. (1995). Enchanted Strong's Lexicon. Woodside Bible Fellowship.
9. "exousia" Merrill, R. (2014) Authority. D. Magnum, D.R. Brown, R. Klippenstein, & R. Hurst (Eds.), Lexham Theological Wordbook. Bellingham, WA: Lexham Press
10. "submit - hypotage" Magnum, D., & Twist, E. T. (2013). 1 Timothy. (D. Mangum & D.R. Brown, Eds.) (1 Ti 2:11). Bellingham, WA: Lexham Press.
11. "5125 - stoma" Swanson, J. (1997) Dictionary of Biblical Languages with Semantic Domains: Greek (New Testament) (electronic ed.). Oak Harbor: Logos Research Systems, Inc.
12. "command" Merriam-Webster.com. Accessed June 10, 2016. http://www.merriam-webster.com/dictionary/command.

Chapter 20 - Battle Plan

1. "5536 - topos" Swanson, J. (1997) Dictionary of Biblical Languages with Semantic Domains: Greek (New Testament) (electronic ed.). Oak Harbor: Logos Research Systems, Inc.